ISBN 978-0-656-34723-0
PIBN 10798633

ption REDUCED to TWO DOLLARS Per Annum in Advance

STABLISHED IN 1840.

THE SOUTHERN
LANTER AND FARMER

DEVOTED TO

griculture, Horticulture, and the Mining, Mechanic and Household Arts.

Agriculture is the nursing mother of the Arts.—XENOPHON.
Tillage and Pasturage are the two breasts of the State.—SULLY.

CH: B. WILLIAMS, - - - - EDITOR AND PROPRIETOR.
WM. L. HILL, - - - - GENERAL AGENT.

New Series. RICHMOND, VA., NOVEMBER, 1868. Vol. II.---No. 11.

CONTENTS:

FERGUSSON & RADY, Printers, 1328 Main Street.

THE SOUTHERN
PLANTER & FARMER,

DEVOTED TO

Agriculture, Horticulture and the Mining, Mechanic and Household Arts.

Agriculture is the nursing mother of the Arts.—XENOPHON.
Tillage and Pasturage are the two breasts of the State.—SULLY.

CH: B. WILLIAMS, . : . . . . EDITOR AND PROPRIETOR.

New Series.   RICHMOND, VA., NOVEMBER, 1868.   Vol. II---No. 11.

Goodwyn Agricultural Club.

Our readers will recollect that in the able address of JOHN C. TAYLOR, ESQ., President of this Club, published in our September number, the subject of *"the supply of humus to our worn soil"* was reserved for the next meeting, with the promise of then presenting his views on that topic, which, "of all others," he regarded as "of the deepest importance." . Right worthily has this promise been redeemed, in the article we now have the pleasure of submitting to our readers as the sequel and complement of the former address.

We have let no opportunity pass unimproved of impressing upon our readers the great importance of associated action, when the ends of successful and progressive development of the industrial and material resources of the country are the objects pursued.

, One of the most obvious advantages of these associations is their fitness as a medium for collecting and disseminating information in respect to the geography, topography, climate, soil, productions, mineral resources, forests, water power, &c., &c., of their respective sections. In the present circumstances of the South, as connected with the imperative necessity of looking to foreign immigration as the means of supplying the demands of the country with a laboring population adapted to its altered condition, there is no agency that would prove more efficient than these clubs, if actively and intelligently employed in setting before the enquiring emigrant the inviting advantages of their respective counties.

- We expect much from the Goodwyn Club in this department of usefulness. Much is also to be expected from the active co-operation of the other Clubs recently formed in the county of Granville. We expect to see this county filled ere long with a thriving and prosperous population partly through their instrumentality. The superior advantages of this section of country—advantages by the way common to the greater part of the States of North Carolina and Virginia—consist of a temperature not unlike that of Italy with her cloudless skies and of a soil adapted to the production—in their highest perfection—of every herb, fruit, vegetable and cereal which grows this side of the tropics. It is also well suited to the cultivation of the grasses, so that stock raising may be profitably combined with tillage. Tobacco, too, is an important staple in the section under consideration. Cultivated on a *moderate scale* with skilled labor, it is likely to prove more profitable than cotton or sugar at the South, while all the advantages of healthfulness are in favor of this section. But we have detained our readers too long from the main subject; we now present them with the following

ADDRESS

Of John C. Taylor, Esq., President of the Goodwyn Agricultural Club of the county of Granville, North Carolina, continued from page 519:

GENTLEMEN,—I will now proceed, by your leave, to submit some thoughts on the subject of reclaiming our worn lands by other means than putrescent manures. Not with the hope of enlightening your minds by advancing anything new, or with which you are not already familiar, but of eliciting your opinions, and especially your experience, as to the means of most certainly and cheaply, if not the most speedily, accomplishing the object. There are but few, if any, theories in agriculture, which it is important for us to know, that are not easily comprehended, or about which there is a difference of opinion. But so many and so various are the conditions and incidents attendant on the successful applications of these theories, the non-observance of any one of which may result in failure and disappointment, as to call for the exercise of the nicest and most discriminating judgment. Hence the advantages of our association in which each member may profit by the information and experience of the whole, whereby we may be said to realize, after a manner, the advantages of combined over individual effort.

The improvement of our lands, and all which relates to them, assume a deeper and more interesting aspect since the emancipation of our slaves. Before that event, we looked upon them for the most part as mere temporary abiding places, until we could settle up our affairs and make arrangements to unite in the stream of emigration to the cotton fields and sugar plantations of the South, which was continually passing from our borders. Now, we regard them as permanent homes, to be not only enriched, but beautified and adorned, that those homes may be made more pleasant. We may now erect substantial steadings, plant orchards, aye, and acorns, too, with the hope that our children and our children's children may enjoy the shade of their majestic growth. And where, in our widely extended territory, is there a region more worthy of improvement? For health and good water, a soil rich by nature and susceptible of unlimited improvement, and under a parallel of latitude the best adapted to develop all the faculties and all the energies of the human mind and body, it is unsurpassed, if equalled, by any other. And to these considerations we may justly add the inferior, but not less tempting inducement it presents, to a money getting spirit.

From the most thorough conviction, grounded on experience, I maintain that the horizontal mode of ploughing is an indispensable basis of any system we may adopt of improving our lands. I would as soon believe the individual who exceeds his income can grow rich, as that our lands, cultivated by any other mode, can be preserved in their fertility. In assuming thus boldly this position, I have reference to their, for the most part, rolling surface, and light, friable texture. I am not unmindful that deep ploughing, say with a four-horse plough run to its extremest depth, might partially prevent the evil. But this would be to convert all but the richest into a caput mortuum; nor are we likely to use such a plough. It is not only the better mode to prevent the soil from being washed away by rains, but it keeps the vegetable matter which may accumulate upon the surface from being carried off, and retains it to be converted into a source of fertility. I may add that it retains the moisture from the rains for a longer period—a consideration worthy of regard, since upon most of our lands there is usually a want of moisture. The observance of the following simple rule, which I found by attention to the details of the process after repeated failures, will be attended with invariable success: First, Mark two rows with the leveling instrument, say fifteen or twenty yards apart, and be carefully observant to run an equal number of furrows on each row thus marked, until the intervening space is filled by the last short row. By observing this rule, we may be less exact in the use of the instrument, for it is the relative position of all the rows to each other, and not the exact horizontal level of each one, (which exists only with those accurately marked by the instrument,) that prevents the rains from accumulating in any one part.

I assume it is an admitted proposition, that land will keep up or hold its own when cultivated in corn, followed the ensuing year by small grain, and suffered to rest the third year without being grazed or run on by stock. The truth of this proposition will be supported by every one who has fairly tested it by experience. Indeed, since the publication of Taylor's Arator, in which the enclosing system is so commended, the subject has been uppermost in the mind of almost every farmer in Virginia and North Carolina, and very many have pursued the rotation long enough to be convinced that by the process lands are not only preserved from exhaustion, but improved in fertility. I give, with entire confidence, my own attestation to their improvement—slow, at best it may be, the improvement being hastened or retarded according to the vitality in the soil and its original fertility. Now, there is scarcely a farm in the county of Granville, which does not contain a sufficient quantity of cultivated land to make the corn and other grains required for its support under this rotation, if due attention is given to apportioning the fields with an eye to that object; that is, of assigning for each year of rotation a third part of the average productive power of the whole, respect being had to fertility and surface. And, as it is presumed that no part is to be run on by stock, the crops being cultivated in several parts of the farm will be attended with no inconvenience. Of course, under such a system, no one would be at the expense of cross fences. In the adoption of this rotation, we will be much facilitated by the diminished demand for corn, having no superfluous slaves to give employment to or to feed; causes which have heretofore prevented the steady and uninterrupted adherence to any rotation. And granting that the lands thereby only retain their fertility—though in that case, if in any, it may be said that "not to go back is something to advance"—we have much for congratulation and encouragement; for their condition may be likened to the man who never exceeds his income, and who ultimately is sure to grow rich. But with an increase of fertility beyond that which we know is not to be obtained under this enclosing system, it is not to be expected that any one will or ought to be content; and as we have a use for our putrescent manures for other purposes, the thought naturally presents itself of resorting to a means of which all of us have been talking for years, but which few of us have practiced even on the smallest scale, namely, the aid of green crops. And here a problem is presented to be solved by us only by the lessons of experience. I know myself from repeated experiments that the pea sowed on land in good heart, and ploughed in before the vines have been blighted by frost, will produce a marked and most unmistakable improvement in the soil—an improvement so remunerative of the cost and labor as to present inducement to the use of it, for that purpose on such lands, to the extent of the limits of the lands, however broad the acres. I can show you instances on my own farm in which scepticism itself will assent to its most profitable result. The pea which produces the most fruit to be turned under with the vines should be selected; but it should be turned under before it matures or ripens. But from the same teachings of experience I can, with nearly the same certainty say, that our poor lands, such as will produce only five or ten bushels of corn to the acre, certainly, I think, only five bushels, the product of vines will be so scant as, either by leaving the ground exposed for a longer period to the sun's rays, or from the poor return they make to the soil, to produce no improvement over and above what would be made by the weeds and grass which spring by nature, if so much. It is a question, therefore, of interesting inquiry to know the lowest degree of fertility of soil which will produce a remunerative growth of vines; and in the case where the land is too poor to be improved by the process, to learn the least quantity of guano or gypsum which will grow them of sufficient luxuriance. If you think I am calling your attention to a matter of too small importance to deserve consideration, let us ride over our growing crops of corn and note the difference in their growth on adjoining acres, or even on the same acre. We will see on portions not perhaps the average in fertility of the whole field, good-sized, perfect ears, and near by, on a greater or smaller surface, a product next to nothing at all; and yet we will know by ocular proof that there is but little difference in the soil of the two sections. That the section producing the good ears had not a particle of fertility beyond what was required to perfect them, and that a covering of compost or good crop of pea vines would have brought up the latter to the fertility of the former, to remain so under judicious management for all time. The practice of improving land by green crops, as also the manufacture and management of manures of every description, may be much facilitated by the labor of those freedmen to be found in every neighborhood who, refusing to make contracts for the year, are ever ready to do a day's or week's work.

This facility of procuring assistance at the prescribed time when it is required, without withdrawing to the loss of the growing crop, the hands occupied in making it is a consideration which we can but regard as particularly fortunate and encouraging.

I shall say nothing of red clover, the Samson of green crops, because its merit as a manure is presumed to be universally known, and because it can be grown only on land in a measure rich, while my attention has been directed to, and I may with truth say my affections have been enlisted in behalf of, the broad surfaces in our every field, whose scanty and fickle vegetation seems to struggle to hide, as with a mantle, their naked sterility. I may say, however, that we have yet much to learn of the condition of soil with respect to fertility, on which clover, with the aid of plaster, will grow of sufficient luxuriance to be remunerative as a green crop.

I hope some of us will experiment with Indian corn the next season as a green manure. From the luxuriance with which it grows, it would probably afford more of the humus so much needed by most of our lands than any other vegetable. It has occurred to me that it may be profitably used as a preparation for tobacco. We know how much that crop is improved in quality and size by the presence of vegetable matter. I know from my own experience that it grows well after a corn crop. An additional motive to test its value as a preparation for tobacco is, that it may hereafter be made to supply the deficiency of our farm-yard manure, on account of our reduced stock of cattle. Sown broadcast at the rate of three or four bushels to the acre, it is recommended to mow them close to the ground, when the stalks have attained sufficient height, and in ploughing them in, to fill the first furrow opened partially with the stalks, scattering over them caustic lime, which quickly decomposes them. The furrow thus prepared will be covered by the next slice, and so on to the end.

Amongst the many vegetables used as green crops buckwheat is enumerated. It is said to grow most kindly on thin land, and is of such quick growth that two crops may be ploughed under in the year. I procured a bushel of the seed the last winter, and planted three-fourths of them on good land in June for seed, with which to experiment the next year. The remainder I sowed the first of August between a growth of pea vines on one side, and the uncultivated land on the other, the whole to be ploughed under at the same time as a preparation for corn, that I may judge of the value of each by comparison. I am, so far, encouraged by the luxuriance of its growth. I have been taught the importance of thick sowing, even so late as June, to keep down the growth of weeds and grass. We have hitherto been successful in attaining the ends to which we have aspired. I have travelled from Cape May to the prairies of Texas; have repeatedly spent weeks at a time in the rich section of Western Alabama, and with an eye ever attentive to the state of agriculture, I can confidently say, that I have never seen a farming community which enjoyed more of the comforts, and decencies, and elegancies of life, than that of Granville and the counties adjoining. We have owed our success to the extent of our tracts of land, and to the remains of our forest lands and those reclaimed by the growth of pine. Without enquiry as to how far the reduced limits of the last two resources suggest the approaching necessity of a resort to other agencies, we have a motive to improve our lands which should never be lost sight of. Our anomalous political condition, in connection with the uncertain results of the emancipation of slavery on our system of labor, causes our lands to sell at the present time, when they can be sold at all, for merely nominal prices. But we already see the golden lining of the pestiferous political clouds which have been so long scowling upon us. The increase of our native population, no more to be drained by emigration, and the certain influx of immigration from abroad, when the superior advantages of our section of country shall be better known, will, it is believed in no long time, so advance in the prices which they will command, as that a prudent economy will prompt to the sale of all, with the exception of a comparatively few acres to be retained as homesteads. Hence the obvious inducement of setting about earnestly to improve those to be retained for cultivation; and hence the care and attention we may bestow on those designed for sale, will be amply remunerated by the enhanced prices they will thereby command.

There is a consideration, gentlemen, underlying the whole question of an improved agriculture of deeper interest than the attainment of the object itself. If, as has been said, "happiness consists in hope realized," in what wider or more lovely field is this heaven-given treasure to be found, than in the substitution of growing fruitfulness, for barren sterility,—than in the daily contemplation of multiplied and multiplying comforts and increasing wealth, in connection with the idea of home and its indearments? In such a field the virtuous heart is ever cheered by occupation as agreeable, as it is profitable, (occupation the more agreeable because in consonance with a law of nature written on the heart); while the mind, as strengthened and invigorated by an onward progress towards the attainment of ends so elevating, bids defiance to moping melancholy, vain regrets, self-reproach and the like black train of despondent emotions which constitute so large a portion of the sum of human wretchedness.   In such a field we come to love the external objects we pursue; and when associated with the converse of friends, and blessed with those domestic ties around which the fibres of the heart entwine, what is there wanting to the fruition of that "Domestic happiness," so beautifully apostrophised by the poet, as "the only bliss of paradise that has survived the fall!"   A mind imbued with the spirit of vulgar prosperity may whisper, "put money in your purses, if in so doing you exterminate your lands."   But this would be to pander to the lust of avarice the most debasing of passions. And here we are reminded of the reverse of the picture so imperfectly presented above.   That there is something demoralizing in a slovenly, exterminating course of agriculture, requires no metaphysical subtlety of disquisition to prove.   Our hearts attest it. Whether it be the absence of the idea of permanency, the life and soul of the endearing associations, themselves so many virtues, that we are wont to connect with home, and with country; or of the support which virtue finds in the invigorating influences of an onward and upward progress; or whether we ascribe it to the deterioration of the mind and heart by sympathy with the decline and depreciation of the external things on which they are engaged, our hearts attest that such a course of agriculture is demoralizing.   I speak it in no vein of levity when I say, that we are worse men while sauntering in discontent, or careless unconcern, over a worn surface of our farms; and that in the resolve, and still more in the effort to resuscitate that surface, we are better men.

Address of Commodore Maury

To the Cadets of the Virginia Military Institute, on occasion of his installation as professor of Physics in that Institution, September 10th, 1868.

YOUNG GENTLEMEN, We are here, novices together, with this difference only between us: you are here in the flower and bloom of youth to be trained and exercised and prepared for the great battle of life; I, a raw recruit, already in the sere and yellow leaf of age to fight it out, "just so."

It is never too late for any of us to form good resolutions; but this, the beginning of a new scholastic year, is peculiarly the time to form them, and to reinforce them with noble aspirations.

Select as your model some one who has risen to eminence from the condition in life in which it has pleased God to place you ; compare yourself continually with the wise and good, and with your fellows; not vaingloriously to see how much better you are than they, but secretly, with meekness and humility, to see how much better they are than you, to discover your own faults and correct them.

There is no educational establishment in the land, and considering its age, I might truly say, in the wide world, that is richer than this with its memories, its traditions and its catalogue of good and great men.

Go to the studio of Mr. Washington, and you will see there in preparation the portraits of our gallant dead, who fell in the war, and who, as teachers and scholars, once graced these halls with their presence. Our superintendent, with affectionate interest and a wisdom of purpose that is beyond praise, is causing a picture gallery to be prepared of these noble spirits, that their memories may be embaled in your hearts, and their virtues and their example treasured up to serve you as guides and models, when the time comes.

This institute, young as it is, furnished the war with a long list of heroes. Good men they were and true, every one of them. When their likenesses are hung in their places, go often to see them. Go with companions, that you may talk of their gallant deeds and noble daring, their Christian virtues and manly graces. But when you feel that your good resolutions begin to fail, go alone, and listen to those eloquent mutes on the canvass, and gather fresh resolution and determined will, by gazing upon the pictures of Jackson and Garland, of Rodes, and Crutchfield, and of their fallen comrades.

Strive in all things and at all times to be right-minded ; and as you are conducted along those beautiful walks in the fields of physical research, which modern investigation has made so lovely and instructive, guard against the seductive arguments of those authors who delight to point out what they call contraditions to the Bible.

My dear young friends, always remember that the author of that Book is nature's God—that the revelations of science and the statements of the Bible are both true, and that truth cannot contradict itself.

Now, when you fancy you discover, as many say they do, discrepancies between science and the Bible, be not fast, as Colenso and others have been, to pronounce the Bible wrong. Keep from presumptious sins, and be firm in the belief that the Bible is true—

that science is true, and that if there be apparent discrepancy between these two records it is not the fault of either, but of yourself, their interpreter. The records are right, but their interpretation has, on many occasions, been wrong.

Science is progressive, and for its healthful advancement speculation is often necessary. The boldness of such speculation, uttered in the shape of hypotheses, has sometimes startled the world, and needlessly disturbed the minds of Christian people. Sometimes the reading of the Bible has been wrong, and sometimes of the volume of nature, but in the end the dark sayings of each have been found to throw light upon the other. Gallileo, in advance of his time, maintained that the earth turns on its axis; and "Mother Church" in those days was offended. She pronounced the doctrine a damnable heresy, and required him to renounce it. As he signed the recantation and turned away, he muttered: "Yea, remember, but it turns for all that." So, too, with the Nebulæ hypothesis, about which you are yet to learn, but which some good men have been disposed to regard as a modern heresy, because of its author. Recent discovery and scientific investigation are now presenting it in a new light, without in the least disturbing any religious belief whatever.   •

First, hypothesis, then theory, then demonstration—these are the steps by which the science of astronomy has reached its present advanced state. At first, the hypothesis was that the earth was the centre of the universe; that it stood still, and that the heavens rolled round it from East to West. But discovery and research soon convinced astronomers that this theory was not consistent with the results of observation. Then, the theory was that the heavens stood still, and that the earth turned around daily on its axis from West to East, and annually, in orbital revolution, round the sun. Observation and research furnished data by which the truth of this theory, as far as it goes, was demonstrated. Finally, it was discovered that the sun is moving through space with the velocity of cannon balls, carrying in his train the earth and the whole retinue of planets, asteroids and satellites, and so hypothesis was brought to the dignity of a theory, which reconciles all the known facts of the case.

Though we may not claim that the Nebulæ hypothesis has, as yet, attained to the dignity of a theory, nevertheless its plausibility appears to be such as to bring it within the range of probability, and, therefore, it may or may not have truth for its corner-stone.

The Nebulæ hypothesis is the conception of a great French

geometer named La Place.   This hypothesis is more profound in its reach than Newton's laws; for the Englishman with his beautiful theory of gravitation only dealt with the heavenly bodies as he found them.   The Frenchman, soaring beyond that, attempted to deal with them "from the beginning," to comprehend chaos and to show how, when the earth was without form and void, the various physical processes took place by which the inorganic matter of the universe was condensed into suns, aggregated into planets, thrown off and converted into satellites, sent wheeling on their orbits about the sun, and then turning on their axes.   In comparing these two philosophers, I speak of their intellects, not of their characters.

You know how all the planets revolve in the same direction, how they go round the sun in a direction opposite to that of the hands of a watch, and have their orbits nearly in the plane of the sun's equator; that they also rotate on their axes in the same direction, and that with the single exception, perhaps, of the two outside, and most distant planets, all their moons do the same.   They could not move as they do by any chance, for there is no chance in nature, neither in the heavens nor in the earth; moreover, according to the doctrine of chances, the odds are millions and millions to one against such an arrangement as that which we actually behold among the planets as they move in their orbits.

It is assumed, as our point of departure, that this arrangement in the planetary world must be according to design and in obedience to law.   Upon other assumptions equally plausible, its author founded his hypothesis, and then proceeded by analogy and illustration to develop it, and that with a degree of probability, which, if it do not carry conviction to our minds, must at least challenge our respect and admiration.   It assumes that "in the beginning" the earth, sun and moon, with all the planets, were in a gaseous state; that when this was the case the planetary spaces were filled by this rare and attenuated matter.

What are the reasons for these assumptions?   Chemistry tells us that all the matter of which this earth consists—the rocks, the metals and the mountains—is made from sixty-one or sixty-two simple substances; that the greater part of all the solid matter in the world is gaseous; that one-half of the earth's crust consists of oxygen alone, and that all the water in the sea is composed of but two gases, and nothing else, and that all the other substances known upon the earth may, by heat, be either volatilized or converted into fumes and vapors, as rare, light and attenuated as the gases themselves.   With such materials, which the Frenchman called *nebulous,* he, with his theory, filled the planetary spaces. That this assumption may receive from you its due weight, it is necessary to state that we have recently discovered, and can now prove almost that the nebulæ are of just such materials as this hypothesis calls for.

As this chaotic mass of matter began—so runs the hypothesis— to radiate off its heat, for the assumption is, (and it is supported by many analogies,) that the centre of our planet is still in an incandescent state—as, therefore, this chaotic and highly-heated mass began to radiate off its heat and to cool, it began to contract, and thus motion was generated from that movement, the hypothesis derives the *primum mobile* or the power which first gave to the planets motion in their orbits.

Such, in brief, are the assumptions of La Place, and, being granted, the rest is philosophical deduction. Newton's laws took no notice of the great first cause that sent the planets wheeling round the sun in their peculiar orbits, and set them all revolving and rotating in the same direction on their axes; nor did his laws attempt to account for the satellites and rings which attend some of the planets.

In going beyond gravity and grappling with first causes and *primum mobile,* the Frenchman stalked forth into dark regions and travelled proudly upon grounds which the Englishman, as great and as gigantic as was his intellet, had not ventured to essay. To explain the nebulæ hypothesis upon the basis of these assumptions, let us avail ourselves of familiar instances for illustration : You have observed, while driving fast along a muddy road, that the carriage wheels throw the mud, not straight off from the carriage to the side of the road, but forward and nearly in the plane in which the wheels turn. If you will watch the larger pieces of mud closely you will discover that they have a rotary motion, like the wheel, and in the same direction. Bearing in mind this homely illustration, let us return to the original nebulous mass. It is highly heated and easier of attraction by being globular in form. Consider it to be at rest and the process of cooling to have commenced, and see when it takes place. The cooling is from the outside, the condensing is consequently on the outside—wherefore a movement commences from the circumference towards the centre, and because it is from the circumference towards the centre it is a rotary motion.

It is such a motion as we see in the whirlwind on land and in the whirlpool in the water. This begets a revolving motion either to the right or to the left, and in the nebulæ of the solar system, it was from the right to the left.   Thus the nebulous mass was set in motion.

As it continued to cool and contract, the outer particles continued to flow inward, and, as in all revolving bodies, the particles at the circumference travel faster than the particles near the centre—these in-rushing particles carried their momentum from the circumference to the centre, impressed it there, and gradually accelerated the revolving motion to such an extent that the centrifugal force at the circumference became greater than the centripedal, and so a lump or a ring was thrown off, first one and then another; for, as the nebulous mass continued to cool and contract, its velocity of rotation continued to increase, and so, first the matter for Neptune and his satellites; then for Uranus, then for Saturn and his rings, was thrown off all in and near the plane in which the great central mass itself was revolving.

These fragments were not thrown off in the solid state, but as liquid or gaseous matter; for we know that Saturn, Jupiter, Mars and the earth are all spheroids, and of such shape as a mass of matter only in the fluid condition revolving about its own axis could assume, and we know that the interior of the earth is still in a fluid state, which is quite consistent with the idea that the whole was once fluid.

Saturn is still in the sky with his rings to attest this mode of sloughing off matter; nor is the sun altogether without them.   These rings—so holds the theory—were afterwards broken up into one or more planets with or without moons—with or without rings; all of which continued to move nearly in the same plane, and to rotate on their axes; they revolve, every one with the exception already mentioned, in the same direction around their primaries.

The stream of asteroids between Mars and Jupiter now stand out under this grand and sublime hypothesis, not as fragments of a broken planet, but as pieces of a severed ring.

The November and August meteors constitute a ring.   The Zodiacal light is also a ring, and some of the most remarkable nebulæ in the sky are rings.   Striking analogies are afforded by some of them in favor of La Place's hypothesis, as the Nebulæ in Canes Venatici with its central agglomeration, its rings and planetary nebulous mass in the distance.

Then again, in Leo, Lord Ross' telescope reveals Nebulæ that make still more plausible the great Frenchman's hypothesis.

In other parts of the sky, and as if to show that nebulæ do grow

into stars and suns, that monster telescope has picked up planetary
nebulæ that are apparently stars in process of formation.

But Saturn presents the most grand and striking example of all,
though we find in the heavens nebulæ of more fantastic forms and
curious shapes than Saturn with his rings and moons.

The close of Commodore Maury's address was followed by general and hearty applause, the cadets giving three cheers, with a real
will for "Lieutenant" Maury. After the congratulations of the
Superintendent and members of the Faculty, Commodore Maury
was introduced to many gentlemen and ladies who had listened with
close attention to his address.

The interesting ceremonies closed with a collation given by the
Superintendent in honor of the occasion.

The Wheat Crop of the United States.

*The Increase in the Production of Wheat Falling Off—A Good
Crop no Longer Results in a Large Surplus and Low Prices.*

There are many facts and reasons in relation to wheat which
show that the increase in production is not keeping pace with the
increase of population and consumption. As many farmers are still
at a loss to understand why a good crop of wheat no longer furnishes
a large surplus, or results in low prices, it may be well to consider
briefly some of the reasons.

In new and remote sections, with limited facility for reaching
markets, there are few products that can be grown and sent to market to so good advantage as wheat. When first brought into cultivation the soil is rich, and wheat is more easily grown than at any
time afterwards. There is also less injury from insects, and the
grain is of better quality. There is no other product that so fully
combines the advantages of a good demand, ready market, and ease
and safety of transportation as wheat. But as the country grows
older, and the land worn, a variety of crops, including a due proportion of animal products, is found best for the land, and most
profitable to the farmer. Then the growth of cities and towns, and
increasing facilities in good roads, canals and railroads, for reaching
distant markets, makes an increasing demand for other products.
This finally results in a large demand for the great variety of products used in rich communities.

In heavily timbered countries, before the advent of railroads, this change was slow. But on the vast prairies of the West, where the pioneer is soon followed by the iron horse, the changes are rapid. For instance—between 1840 and 1850 the increase of the wheat crop was only from 84,821,065 to 1C0,485,944 bushels; while in 1860 it had increased to 173,104,924. This is an increase of not quite 18½ per cent. in the first ten years, while it is 72 per cent. during the latter decade. This great difference is mainly due to the rapid settling and bringing into cultivation of the prairies.

This increase was very large for a year or two longer ; then there was a turn in the scale, and the amount fell off. This continued until 1866, when there was but little more, if, indeed, there was as much grown, as there was in 1859 ; although the rate of increase for ten years previous to the latter date, if realized, would bring the crop of 1866 up to about 242,000,000 bushels. During the same time the increase in population was over 7,000,000, requiring, at five bushels each, and including seed, some 40,000,000 bushels more wheat for the current year. So there will be little surprise that the exports of wheat, and flour calculated as wheat, at five bushels to the barrel, fell off from rising 60,000,000 for the crop of 1861, to 3,633,338 bushels for the crop grown in 1866. What allowance should be made for wheat grown the previous year, in each case, there is no way to ascertain ; but it is well known the crop of 1866 was very closely used up at the next harvest—in 1867—much more so than any previous year, so we may safely conclude the surplus was very small.

There are many reasons for this falling off in the rate of increase. The war, insects of different kinds, and unfavorable seasons, have all had some effect ; but peace, a favorable season, and high prices, failed to secure a very large increase or heavy surplus for export in 1867, as was formerly the case. Hence the principal reason for this change must be found in the change of farming referred to, which has largely taken place in those States at the West where there had previously been the greatest increase.

The attentive reader of the *Country Gentleman* has seen, in the numerous letters from the West, many accounts of and reasons for this change. B. F. J. has given full and graphic accounts of the change from small to large farms, and the consequent change from wheat to corn and stock farming in Central Illinois. Similar changes are taking place in other sections of the West. Wheat becoming a rather uncertain and expensive crop, farmers there, as everywhere else, find it better to grow a variety of crops and animal products. The rapid increase of railroads, by affording facilities.for moving these products to distant markets, contributes largely to this change; and the unparalleled increase in number and size of Western cities and towns, by making local markets for bulky crops (like hay, potatoes and vegetables,) as well as dairy products and the great variety of large and small fruits now so largely used, has also led to a greater variety in farming.

But perhaps there is nothing that has so much influence on the comparative amount of wheat grown, as the fact that there are no new States or Territories sufficiently large, fertile and productive, to take the place of the great wheat-producing States in the West, now changing to general farming. During the past twenty years these States have grown an immense amount of wheat; but the main portion of their best lands is under cultivation, and in all but the newer sections wheat is gradually giving place to other crops. So we cannot expect to keep up the increase heretofore realized, without the addition of new States equally productive. Indeed, there is much reason to fear we shall fail to keep the increase in production up to the ratio of the increase in population, without such help.

It will hardly answer to say we can do it by better farming; for better farming means a rotation of crops, and less wheat than is usually grown on new land. It will give a larger yield per acre; but does not admit of sowing so many acres. The example of England is very instructive on this point. Up to a comparatively recent period, wheat was grown there for export; and grown, too, without the aids and advantages of modern farming. But as popu-lation increased, and a larger portion used wheat bread, consump-tion gained steadily on production, until with all the help of modern scientific farming, by which the yield of wheat per acre has been more than doubled, and large sections, before useless, have been made to grow wheat, they no longer raise their bread, but have to im-port from twenty-five to seventy-five or eighty millions of bushels a year.

Now there is the same tendency here—not that we shall soon have to import wheat, but that we can no longer keep up the great ratio of increase until recently realized. We may make great im-provements in farming; but a large yield of wheat, to be perma-nently and profitably secured requires a suitable rotation of crops and high manuring. This confines wheat to a rather small portion of the farm each year, and cannot here, any more than in England, make the increase in production keep pace with the increase in population.

Meantime the improvements in farming, that secure better yields of wheat, are very slowly adopted. Much of our best wheat lands are still cropped on the exhausting system. Many of the older States are falling off in the amount of wheat grown, although still increasing in population. This the new States are no longer able to supply, and still keep the average increase up to former years; while the older portions of these States are changing to other crops, and less wheat, with no corresponding increase of new land brought into cultivation. Not but a great deal of new land is broken up every year, but that there is not enough to take the place of older lands in wheat-growing, and also to keep up the large rate of increase heretofore expected.

And then the increase in population is a great deal larger now— being from 476,965 a year in 1840, to 1,135,180 a year in 1867. This increase requires an addition of five or six million bushels of wheat a year, and is constantly growing. Where can we look for the new States that are able to supply these increasing demands, and furnish the usual increasing supplies for export besides? California, though doing well, cannot do it; the increasing demands of a few Eastern States will soon absorb all that State has to spare, while the increase in the foreign demand will more than offset any increase we can expect on the Pacific Coast. Canada has furnished considerable wheat; bnt it is quite likely that, since the end of reciprocity, and the addition of twenty-five cents duty (in gold) per bushel, we will get much less wheat from there.

But enough at this time. By the foregoing will be seen why we no longer grow the large surplus expected when we had a fair crop of wheat, and why with such a crop, wheat is all wanted at good prices.—*F., in Cultivator and Country Gentleman.*

Premium Essay.

The premium offered by the Central Agricultural Society of Granville, Warren and Franklin counties, N. C., for the best essay on "*The Culture, Curing and Subsequent Management of Bright Yellow Tobacco,*" was awarded to Dr. Thomas P. Atkinson, of Danville, Va., at the late fair of the Society, held at Henderson, on the 14th, 15th and 16th of October, 1868.

We are indebted to the promptness and courtesy of W. W. Young, Esq., Chairman of the Executive Committee of the Society, for the privilege of presenting his essay so early in the pages of our journal. Granville makes a good start in the race of agricultural improvement and progress; may she press towards the mark and run with patience till she wins the prize, and is crowned with peace and plenteous prosperity.

Essay on the Cultivation, Curing and Subsequent Management of "Bright Yellow Tobacco."

Whilst much of what I shall write will be applicable to the treatment of tobacco in general, I shall treat specially of the proper mode of growing, curing and management of the high priced *yellow wrapping tobacco*, which commands, in our principal markets, almost fabulous prices, for to this, chiefly, must our planters look to enable them to meet expenses and to pay for their clothing and groceries.

There are but few of them who can afford to make the ordinary shipping tobacco, whilst they shall be subject to the present high taxes and to all the evils consequent on free labor; hence the necessity of turning their attention to producing the only kind which will amply remunerate them for the outlay and the labor required to make it.

The first thing to be looked to in growing tobacco is to *provide plants enough* to "*pitch the crop*" in good time, before the summer's sun shall have so completely evaporated the moisture from the ground as to require frequent showers to insure "a *good stand.*"

Inattention to this all-important requisite often causes a failure of the crop, and leads the planter to complain of Providence when, in fact, *he only* is to be blamed.

I remember to have met, nearly fifty years ago, in the city of Petersburg, the celebrated John Randolph, of Roanoke. It was in the month of June, and he inquired of me if the planters in my neighborhood had finished pitching their crops. On being told that there had been no rain since the plants had become large enough to be removed, and that but a small portion of the crop had been planted, he exclaimed: "Bad management, sir, bad management! I have no sympathy for the planter who fails to make a crop from any such cause. I always *have my plants grown in time* and *my hills made when the ground is in moist order*, and *never wait for a season.*" "Any one (he continued) who shall always manage thus, may cut off his hills and plant any time before the 20th of May, with a fair prospect of having a good stand."

Mr. Randolph was a practical and a successful planter on a large scale, and his suggestions deserve to be well heeded by all tobacco growers.

But the question arises, "how shall we insure plants in good time?" The best plan, in my judgment, is to

Select your plant ground in April. Look rather to *the texture* than to the fertility of the soil. A spot in the woods, where the land is of a *soapy* appearance, neither too stiff nor too light, but with a due admixture of sand and near the base of a declivity, looking towards the south or southeast, is to be preferred.

Make *your cow-pen* on the ground thus selected, and keep your cattle upon it *until it shall be made very rich;* then remove them to another place chosen as above, and so on from point to point until you shall have manured ground enough to raise plants sufficient for your own crop, with many left for your less provident neighbors. When you remove the cattle from one of these places, cut down the bushes and trees from it, cover the ground thickly with the brush to protect it from the sun, split the wood and throw the limbs on the brush, stack the wood near the place, so as to allow it to dry.

As soon as you shall have finished housing your corn in November, set fire to the brush and limbs; and having previously prepared wood for burning the ground, perform that operation in the usual way. If you will do this when the *ground is dry,* you will accomplish the work in little more than half the time, and with but little more than half the wood required by the ordinary mode of proceeding in the winter, after the land shall have become saturated with water, when a large portion of the wood is consumed *in drying the land.*

On the plan recommended, all this is saved; for you will find that the land will be dry when you start the fire. The saving of labor and fuel thus effected is an object of no small consideration.

As soon as the ground shall have been sufficiently burned, rake off the coals and *coalter it very deep both ways* with a sharp, narrow coalter; then rake it carefully, *taking care to get out all the loose roots;* spread over it a moderate quantity of guano, lay it off in beds four feet wide, trench the ground properly around the patch, so as to prevent the outside water from passing through it, and fence it in.

Having thus prepared it as nicely as if you intended to sow it *then,* leave it until the first snow in December, when you should scatter your seed regularly over the white surface, in the proportion of two table-spoonfuls to one hundred square yards.

As soon as the land shall be dry enough, after the melting of the snow, *tread it firmly,* and cover it thickly with *the fine dust from a coal kiln*, over which a thick coat of fine straight brush should be thrown.

The coal dust being *black* is an absorbent of heat, and thus keeps the ground warmer than it would otherwise be, and so pushes the plants forward. The warmth thus produced by the *black surface* may be demonstrated to the satisfaction of any one who will place strips of cloth of black and other colors on the snow. It will be found *that the snow under the black strips will be melted before that under either of the others.*

I have advised that the plant land shall be selected about the *first of April.* If the cattle be put upon it before, whilst they are fed on wheat or oat-straw, or hay of any kind, the seeds from these articles will be deposited on the ground in the manure, and springing up amongst the plants will prove very troublesome. By beginning to manure thus early, the process may be completed before the seeds of the grass shall be matured, and thus another trouble will be avoided.

If there be no snow in December, the seed should be sown about the first of January, and the ground well trodden when dry and otherwise treated as above recommended.

He who will try the coaltering process will be astonished at the great number of roots which will be extracted, and which, if left in the ground, serve only to keep it open, and thus to expose the delicate plants to be destroyed by the frost. He will also be gratified to find that the deep and close breaking of the land will *keep the ground moist in dry weather*, which will destroy the plant in beds treated in the usual way and *scratched with a grubbing hoe or mattock.*

About the first of March the beds should be resown with about *half the quantity of seed* used in the first sowing—"*the broad leaf Oronoko*" is preferred by most of our good planters in this neighborhood, which is famed for producing the finest tobacco in the world, and in which I am satisfied that more money has been made to the hand, for the last ten or fifteen years, since the present mode of curing has been introduced, than on the sugar or cotton plantations of the Gulf States.

The freezing process through which the land must necessarily pass in winter, and by which the plants are often thrown on or near the surface and destroyed, will be much less injurious under the management here recommended than any other.

Whenever the ground is thus affected by the freezing, the beds should be uncovered and kept down by passing over them, as often as may be required, a heavy roller made of gum or other heavy wood. After each rolling, they should be *again covered with coal dust* before the brush is returned to them. Plant beds treated in this way may be safely relied on to furnish a full supply of *good* plants in time to pitch the crop by the 15th of May, at which time the provident planter will have his ground ready to receive them.

Old land, *intended for tobacco,* should be ploughed deep and close, early in September, before the vegetation on it shall have been killed by frost, *taking care to cover all such matter well.* I prefer to throw it into *high beds,* three feet four inches apart, so as to allow the winter's water to pass off freely and the frost to permeate fully.

About the 10th of April the beds should be ploughed down, and as soon thereafter as it shall become sufficiently moist, from 200 to 250 pounds of the best Peruvian Guano should be sown evenly over it, and new beds thrown up the same distance apart as before. Before putting on the guano, the ground should be well harrowed with an iron tooth harrow.

As soon as the plants shall have attained to the proper size for setting out, these ridges should be cut off *much lower than is usual amongst planters,* and firmly beaten down with the back of the hoe. The proper distance between the plants is three feet, and to insure uniformity in this, each of the hands should have it marked on his hoe-helve. A gray, soft soil is greatly to be preferred, as it is difficult to make the tobacco ripen yellow on a stiff soil.

Land which has been long "turned out" and allowed to grow up with "old-field pines" is best.

I have recommended that the plants shall be set into the ground lower than is usual. An experience of sixteen years in the cultivation of tobacco on a pretty extensive scale, and a much longer observation of the operations of other planters, has convinced me that they are always *planted too high on upland.* I know that in *their advanced stage,* when the suckers make their appearance, the great object of the planter should be *to protect them from too much moisture ;* but whilst young, they require more rain than corn does in like condition. This last named plant, although it demands much moisture *whilst earing,* can do with but little when very small.

It is just the reverse with tobacco, which *requires frequent showers to start it to grow,* but *cannot stand* much *wet whilst it is maturing.* Every planter knows that in the usual way of planting, the tobacco will remain stationary for weeks, (if it does not die,) unless the rain shall come soon after it is put into the hill.

Hence the propriety of setting it lower in the ground than is usual, and making the hill in the progress of cultivation, so that by the time it shall receive the last working, *there shall no loose dirt* be left between the hills by which the free passage of the water may be obstructed.

I would allow no one to hill my old upland, intended for tobacco, although it might be offered to be done without compensation. The advantage of beds over hills is found in the fact that, from the beds, the evaporation is *from only two sides*, whilst from the hills it is from the entire circumference. Hence we find that unless there be frequent showers shortly after planting, the tender and, in this stage of its being, *the thirsty plant* is often not larger at the end of two or three weeks than it was at the time it was set out. The crop is thus kept back much to its injury and often to its entire destruction by frost.

He who shall try the plan of planting in beds and setting the plants lower in the ground than he has been accustomed to do, taking care to convert the beds into hills as he shall cultivate, will never revert to his old and ruinous custom of depriving his young plants of moisture AT A TIME *when they most need it.*

Let me repeat what I have already said, that whilst corn requires but little moisture while it is very young *and demands a great deal when maturing*, tobacco needs it most whilst young, and is greatly injured by too much after it shall have passed the topping stage. Hence, the object of the planter should be to adapt his system of culture to the wants of each, protecting the tobacco from the effects of too much wet in its advanced stage, and soliciting for the corn the greatest amount of moisture that the earth, *deeply and closely* ploughed, can be induced to yield.

It can scarcely be necessary for me to say that new ground, or very fresh land, is best adapted to the growth of yellow tobacco, which always commands the highest price in every market. Indeed, none other can be safely relied on for this purpose.

In clearing the land, it is important that it shall be *well grubbed*, and after having been thoroughly coaltered both ways, it should be well ploughed with a bull-tongue or narrow shovel plough, and as many roots as possible removed.

The coal for curing should be prepared in the new ground, in sufficient quantity, to allow from seventy-five to one hundred bushels to each curing of a barn of twenty feet square. This should be securely placed away in a house prepared for the purpose near each barn, so *as to keep it perfectly dry.*

I should have mentioned above that, in planting, great care should be taken in pressing the dirt closely *around the roots*, unless the ground be quite wet, in which case the pressure should be light.

About the first of May the planter should begin to plant and keep his hands at it, *during every evening*, until the crop shall be pitched.   Let the new ground hills be cut off low, for the same reason already assigned in the case of *old upland*, which last should be *first planted*. .

The cultivation of new and old land should be different.   The first should be *scraped* down with a sharp hoe, as soon as the plants have started to grow, when great care should be taken not to loosen the dirt around their roots, whilst all weeds which may have sprung up should be destroyed.   A second working is all that will be required.   This should be effected by about three furrows made with a shovel plough, and the dirt thus loosened should be made into large round hills about the plants.

The first working of "OLD UPLAND" should be by running the bar of a single Dagon plough next to the plant, throwing the dirt into the middle of the row, and thus covering what grass may be there. Only a slight hoeing will be required at this time.   At the second working the land should be well ploughed with a sharp shovel plough, and all the loose dirt should be carefully piled around the plants, so as to leave none in the rows to odstruct the free passage of the water, as at this stage much wet will prove very injurious to the crop.

Up to this point the directions have been definite and precise. Those which will follow must *necessarily* be contingent and general, as the same treatment will no more suit every case than it will in treating the diseases of the human system.   Much must, therefore, be left to the discretion of him who shall manage each case; and it may be well to say at once, that the inexperienced planter will as often be at a loss how to proceed as will be the conscientious beginner in the practice of medicine.   Both should avail themselves of the counsel of their more experienced brethren, whenever it can be obtained.

I would advise him who proposes to enter on the raising and curing of yellow tobacco, to watch closely the management of his most successful neighbors, before engaging in so hazardous an enterprise; nor should he be content with this; but he should employ some person skilled in the business to cure his first crop.   In this way he may, by close personal attention and observation, learn for himself, and thus become an expert at the business.

This is as important to the curer of yellow tobacco as instruction is at the bedside of the sick is to a practitioner of medicine.

Without the one the planter will spoil many of his first cured barns of tobacco, and without the other the physician will lose many of his first patients.

All that can be done by the instructor in either business, is to give *general directions*, leaving it to the pupil to adapt the treatment to circumstances of each particular case that shall come under his treatment; for, in both, *it is practice only which can insure success.*

With this understanding, I submit the following

General Directions

for the curing and subsequent management of bright yellow tobacco:

As soon as the plant *begins to button* it should be *carefully topped* to ten or twelve leaves, according to the fertility of the soil upon which it is grown. To insure a *rich leaf*, it is better to top *too low than too high.*

It is at this point that the responsibility of the practitioner above alluded to commences, for here *no little judgment is required.* The crop should be carefully *wormed* and *suckered,* at least once in each week, and as much oftener as other pressing engagements shall allow.

There is as much difference between ripe and green tobacco as *between ripe and green fruit.* The cutting should not be commenced, therefore, *until the plant shall be fully matured;* and here again the *judgment must govern the action. Tobacco should never be cut* whilst it is wet with *dew* or *rain,* if we desire it to cure readily and well.

Before giving directions for curing, I should not omit to say that it is very important that the barns *shall be tight,* and well protected from the wet which springs out of the ground, by *careful trenching* and *embankment around* the *outside of the building,* and by having the floors to incline slightly to the centre from each direction.

Before hauling the tobacco from the field, it should be properly *sorted,* taking care to place together only those plants *of like size and appearance* to go to the same barn. This uniformity is of great importance to make it appear well in market; for it has no little influence *in determining the price* which it will bring when offered for sale.

Another matter of importance to be attended to is to have a

suitable room for packing the tobacco, after stripping. For this purpose, I would have a room twelve feet wide, to be proportioned in length and height to the quantity of the article raised, located convenient to, but not *connected with the* barn, so as to involve a risk of having it burned in case of the destruction of the latter by fire.

This room should be ceiled and floored with well seasoned plank. A row of studs should be extended from the floor to the ceiling, three feet from each side of the room, which shall have a window with bars opposite to the door.

In packing down the tobacco, place a dry plank on the inside of these studs, with one edge on the floor; against this plank and ceiling, butt the heads of the bundles previously straightened, by having them passed through the hands, lapping the tails in the middle; raise the plank as the process of packing may require, until that side of the passage shall be filled, when the other side may be treated in the same way; nail strips on the outer side of these studs, against which tobacco sticks should be placed setting one end on the floor, and between the stick and the tobacco insert *dry* straw or *hay* (the latter is to be preferred), so as to *protect* the *heads of the bundles from mould.* Cover the bulk *with dry* plank and weight it heavily, and the tobacco, if in good order when packed down, will preserve its order as well as if packed in a hogshead, and when taken out to be prized, will be *straight* and neat in appearance.

The floor of this room should be far enough from the ground to allow a free circulation of air underneath it, so as to protect the tobacco from moisture.

With this preparation of barns, packing house and coal, you may proceed to

Housing the Crop.

From seven to eight plants (according to size) should be put at equal distance upon a stick, and placed on the tiers about six or eight inches apart.

Having filled the barn, string the leaves which may have been broken from the stalks, and have the floor properly swept.

In about twenty-four hours the

Firing

may be commenced. At this stage of the business, the utmost vigilance and caution and the exercise of the best judgment are required. As before remarked, the operator should not be tied down by any rigid rule to be observed in every specific case. If he be without the skill which will enable him to adapt the treatment in regulating the degree of heat as the process of curing shall advance, he will miss the mark, and his effort will be more or less a failure, the injury of which can be avoided only in his future experiments.

With a *good thermometer* suspended on the lowest tier, about the middle of the barn, he may commence his charcoal fires in rows four feet apart, and four fires in a row.

With a heat ranging from eighty-five to ninety-five degrees, the stem will be withered ordinarily in from twelve to twenty-four hours.

At this stage commence the *steaming process*, by raising the mercury a degree every quarter ·of an hour, until it shall rise to about 105.

Watch closely, and if the tobacco remain dry and *begins to curl at the ends,* increase the heat to 110°. It will not be sufficient that the tobacco *on the* bottom tiers shall be dry. It *should be so throughout* the barn. The condition of that on the upper tiers may be ascertained by feeling it with a stick kept for that purpose.

It may be as well to state here, that more time will be required to carry the tobacco through the several processes recommended in wet weather, when the stem and stalk are supplied with an unusual quantity of sap. The exact time of raising the heat, as well as the degree to which it shall be carried, *must be controlled by the judgment of the curer.* If, in the course of five hours, the tobacco continue dry, raise the heat ten degrees higher. If, however, there be much sweat, *the fires should be pulled down and the door opened* for a time, until the sweat shall disappear.

As in the diseases to which our physical frames are subject, there are *critical periods,* so in the curing of tobacco; and one of these occurs just at this point, for the fairest prospect for a house of bright yellow tobacco may be blasted by a mistake of a few degrees of heat. Having dried the tobacco, the heat should be raised to 120 degrees, which will soon cure the leaf; when this shall have been effected, increase the heat to about 160°, and keep it at that point until the stem and stalk be thoroughly cured.

If any sap be left in the stalk, it will run back into the leaf and turn it red. Hence the importance of seeing that *the stalk* as well as the stem be thoroughly cured before stopping the fires.

When the tobacco shall be cooled and become in order to be handled, it should be removed to a dry barn and stored away nicely and *closely* to protect it from the effects of damp and windy weather.

Should a long rainy spell occur, raise a small coal fire under it, so as to dry it completely. A neglect of this will greatly endanger its color, and the planter will find that what he placed in the barn as an article of bright yellow color, will be taken out looking as red as a piece of well-tanned red sole leather.

When it comes in order for stripping, it should be taken down and placed in bulk.

In stripping, the operator should be very careful to put leaves of *like color and length* in *the same bundle.* These should be *small*, hung on drawn sticks, and returned to the tiers. About twenty-five bundles should be placed on a stick and the sticks *hung close* and *never allowed* to become *high in order.* Too much care cannot be observed in sorting as to size and color, or in keeping the tobacco in dry order, during the winter and spring, until it shall be struck down for prizing. This should be done during the prevalence of a *southern wind,* and when the stem will break on a slight bending—while the leaf shall be pliable and soft. Packed down in this condition, and in the manner above recommended, the planter need fear no change of color in the article.

In prizing, either in hogsheads or tierces, it should not be subjected to a very heavy weight, as, *if it be made to stick together too closely*, the sale will be greatly injured.

I have given these *general directions* in as few words as possible. I would not close this essay without again cautioning the inexperienced curer of the high priced yellow tobacco against the delusion of supposing that he can succeed in his first efforts without *some expert* to instruct him in the process of curing. He may save the cost of procuring such a guide in the increased price which he may obtain in *the sale of one barn of tobacco.*

"WALTER RALEIGH."

The Border Agricultural Fair.

We are indebted to the extraordinary enterprise of the *Richmond Dispatch* for the reception of a copy of Ex-Governor Z. B. Vance's address, the morning after its delivery in Danville on the 20th of October, 1868.

The attendance at the Fair was estimated at over five thousand persons, who were entertained with an eloquent introductory address by President Sutherlin. At the conclusion of the President's speech, the orator of the day was introduced, by him, to the multitude present, when he proceeded to deliver the annual address before the Society, as follows:

One of the prettiest stories of the ancients is that of Faith and Confidence displayed by the Romans in selling the ground on which Hannibal was encamping his victorious battalions, jubilant with the slaughter of the consul and his mighty army! Another is told of a brave and self-possessed naval officer the deck-sides of whose ship had been newly painted. During a storm a great wave struck the vessel, threw her on her beam's end, and amid the wild and nervous confusion of the crew, who thought she was going down, he sprang on deck and shouted louder than the roar of the tempest, "Take care, don't touch the paint!" Your great assemblage here to-day reminds me of them. Amid the indescribable desolation of our country, in spite of the financial ruin which has impoverished us, notwithstanding the public calamity and the private sorrow; even amid the fierce throes of this mighty conflict, which in a few short days will perhaps determine the existence or non-existence of constitutional government in America—the noblest labor of the world's noblest men—you have the courage to hold this great meeting of four days to promote the most blessed and peaceful avocations of man! Such is your sublime faith in the future; such your confidence in the heads and hearts of the American people! It is cheering to the last degree. I hail it with ominous gladness. It seems, indeed, as a foretaste of that peace and rest which I trust God has in store for this weary and sorrowing land, and that He is about to make us glad according to the days wherein *He* has afflicted us.

What can I say to-day to add interest to the occasion or promote the great objects of your Society? Instruction in the practical operations of the field, the forest, or the mine, you doubtless scarcely expect. My life having been devoted to other pursuits, my observations of these matters have been made from a standpoint *outside of the fence;* and I believe in all time *a shade farmer* has been held in small esteem by his fellows! Eschewing, then, any attempt to discuss things of which I necessarily know little, the reflections which I have thrown together for the occasion will be altogether of a general and philosophical character.

The first thing that strikes me as worthy of your grave consideration is the great change, in many respects, which the abolition of slavery has brought to Southern farms and farmers. First, it strikes a deadly blow at the system of great farms which prevailed amongst us. The tendency, already visible, will be to break up the vast domains of the Southern planter into small farms, which, with increasing population and agricultural knowledge, will divide and sub-divide into still smaller ones. As this will be caused by the freeing of the negro, it will certainly re-act upon him; for as he breaks up the large farms, the small farms will break him up and drive him from the country by the inevitable substitution of free labor. I take it that these two results will logically follow each other. I do not know that free black labor is employed anywhere in the world where it is possible to obtain the white. The first consequence of the small farm system will certainly be a large increase in the production, in the value of real estate, a rapid improvement in the methods of culture, and increase in the profits of agriculture generally. This, I presume, no well informed man will venture to doubt. So long ago as the days of Cato the Senator, and the poet Virgil, the principle was recognized, as we find both concurring in the maxim, "that it was a grand point in husbandry not to have too much land in one farm, for they considered that more profit came by holding little and tilling it well."

Whilst this beneficent result is thus sure to attend the introduction of the small-farm system, I trust I may be pardoned for remarking that it will nevertheless scarcely be an unmixed good. Man is the creature of his surroundings, and the abolition of the great farms will work a change in him—gradually but surely. That princely hospitality, that domestic refinement, that high social cultivation, that political acumen—the result of wealth and uninterrupted leisure—the nursing mother of a wise and glorious statesmanship: that pure conservatism which was the sheet-anchor of republican liberty; that large-hearted generosity, that honest pride of family and country, which is the basis of a nation's glory; that female excellence, the most charming that ever graced the homes or blessed the hearts of men; for all of which Virginia and the Carolinas were famous the world over. All these will change and measureably disappear. No man can contemplate it without sorrow, if it *is* done in the doubtful name of progress. And when this intelligent class of large land-holders—this sturdy dynasty of democratic kings—is overthrown, history will be compelled to note that the strongest pillar of American civilization, the staunchest supports of American liberty, perished. There is danger, too, of a moral contraction and *narrowing* of our Southern character, and that our people, in their changed condition, will embrace the idea so universally *worshipped* in *progressive* communities—that money is the god of this life, and the accumulation of it the chief end of man! God forbid that these people should ever be bound to the chariot wheels of Ben Franklin, and learn to esteem his picayune maxims above the apothegms of Bacon! May they never, *never* establish a mecca of Cape Cod, or cause the odor of Weathersfield onions to ascend from their altars of sacrifice! Let us hope, and so teach our children, that we may not pass from one extreme of unthrifty extravagance to the other of penurious meanness. I regard this as a real danger, for our people to guard against. It *can* be avoided, and it *should* be avoided. In our zeal to *progress*, to improve our farms and grow rich, let us be careful to remember the *true objects* of life, and the wise lessons of our fathers in regard to them, the culture of *high spirit* and *nobility of soul* in our people!

The change of labor is equally pregnant with important results to our people. The small farmers in our midst never used much negro labor when they could control it as slave. They will utterly repudiate it whenever they can command a better. A demand for white labor is the beginning of immigration, and the beginning of immigration is the beginning of the end of the negro, though that end is not yet. Competition will not spur him into energetic action. It has never yet done so, and never will. He never, under any circumstances, labored with sufficient energy to produce anything beyond the merest subsistence except as a slave. Little did his liberators know, and less care, that in freeing him they removed the only barrier that protected him from the inflowing tide of white civilization, beneath whose waves he must perish; that his liberty was his doom. The political privileges accorded him will only hasten his ruin by increasing his idleness and filling him with dissatisfaction toward the humble paths of labor for which he is fitted. He is told that he should not only control the destinies of a great nation at the ballot-box, but that he is eminently qualified—without knowing the alphabet from a steam engine—to frame the organic laws of a people whose statesmanship is enriched with the experience of 4,000 years! Of course, he cannot be expected to have more sense or honesty than those who tell him these things, and he believes them, and so is spoiled as a laborer. Notwithstanding, too, the vain attempts to overcome it by legal—or rather illegal—enactments, the social repugnance to the black man will increase, and the disposition to employ him will be less than ever. This will be the natural result of the development of his vices and half-suppressed barbarism—the restraining hand of his master being removed—greatly increased, as the feeling will be, by the exposed position of antagonism to the whites into which he has been forced, and for which he is really not to blame. We have no hatred to the blacks—quite the contrary is the real feeling of all who once owned them as slaves. We, therefore, have no desire to supplant them as laborers if their labor could be rendered as profitable as ony other. But so far it has proved a decided failure, at least in the main departments of industry. It is our interest to try that of the white man. If the negro will spur up and compete successfully with the race, then he will be retained; otherwise, he will go down before it—that is all. It is a simple proposition, and will be decided by the law of supply and demand, like all other matters of human industry.

So much for black labor. Having determined that it is best for us to try white, the question arises, Where, when, and in what quantities shall we introduce it, and how shall we get it? Evidently there is a fitness of things which should never be lost sight of. First, What kind of a climate and soil have we, and what do we desire to produce as most profitable? When we understand this we will have an idea where to go for immigration, leaving the other questions, *How* to get it started to us, and how to introduce it?—the greatest ones of all yet to be answered.

Perhaps no land in the world is more favored in regard to climate than is the territory composed within the borders of these two as States. In the very centre of the temperate zone, they as nearly avoid the extremes of heat and cold as it is possible to conceive; and with a surface gently inclining from the white sands of the Atlantic until it imperceptibly swells, on these western borders, into six-thousand-feet elevation, even that equible temperature can be changed or modified at the pleasure of their citizens. Starting from among the ricefields and palmetto forests at the mouth of the Cape Fear, and going directly west, the traveller will pass, before he reaches the tops of the mountains, through climates exactly similar to those of North Carolia proper, Virginia, Pennsylvania, New York and Canada—five hundred feet of elevation being considered equal to a degree of latitude. So varied is the climate of North Carolina—and that of Virginia is scarcely less so—that I believe her productions filled every column for enumeration of American industry in the forms of the census taken in 1860, with the single exception of the West India sugar-cane. The soil of these two great States is equally various. The rich alluvial land of the coast;

the vast swamps, with their interminable forests of cypress; the light, sandy belt of the stately long-leaved pine, marking the ancient shores of a pre-Adamite ocean; then comes the clay and gravel of the undulating mid-lands; then succeeds the granite soils of the Piedmont and mountain country intermingling with carboniferous formations toward the west of the trans-montane section. Of course such a varying soil in such a varying climate will yield almost any class of productions. The husbandman has only to choose what he will grow.

Of the soil of these States I conceive the following general remarks may be made: 1st, That in their virgin state they are at least equal in fertility to the soils of Europe, which feed seven times our population to the square mile. Secondly, That relatively the soils of this country are still in their virgin state—those of Europe having been in cultivation over a thousand years, ours not over one hundred, whilst much the larger portion, say three-fourths, is altogether untouched. Thirdly, That our cultivation being, properly speaking, no cultivation at all, but a mere skimming of the surface without deep ploughing or drainage, the true riches of our soils are unimpaired, or nearly so. Fourthly, Therefore, our "old fields," as our abandoned and supposed to be worn-out lands are termed, having been tilled only to the depth of a few inches, and only damaged by the consumption of the humus, which a judicious application of one or two leguminous or green crops will restore, are generally as valuable as forest soils, when the labor of clearing and bringing the latter into cultivation are considered; the only lands which are permanently injured being those which have been denuded by washing rains, &c.—a very small per cent. indeed.

Thus highly favored both in soil and climate, what shall we produce mainly? With sincere diffidence I shall offer a few suggestions in this regard:

In a country so sparsely settled as ours, and where lands are held in such large bodies, the theory of a division of labor is not sound economy in farming operations. Every farm should be as nearly independent and self-supporting in all respects as it can possibly be made. In mercantile parlance, a farmer should, if possible, be a *general dealer* to at least the extent of his own consumption. Planting, therefore, as contradistinguished from farming—by which we understand a special devotion to cotton, rice, tobacco, or any great staple—is liable to this objection, it is not self-sustaining. An imperfect and unwise arrangement, that is, by which so many of our planters expend the proceeds of their staple crops for provisions and stock, thus paying double profits and commissions, as well as shipping away the fatness of their soils every year and placing nothing back in lieu of it.   Every man who tills the soil as a means of living should surely first provide himself with everything which his farm will grow before he plants a single seed for sale.   Another great objection to planting, or special farming, is that it is ruinously destructive to fertility and an enemy to the improvement of lands. It is, I believe, an accepted truth that there are no means of permanent improvement in our soils equal to the cultivation of some of the grasses and the rearing of flocks, which both *retain* and *return* fertility of the earth.   We are here directly on the dividing line between the *planting* and the *grazing* regions of the United States, and by a judicious and scientific intermingling of *both*, I give it as my unhesitating opinion that we stand in a better position to secure wealth by agricultural means than any other people on the continent.

To successfully develop the agricultural wealth of our country, I deem it not only necessary to reform our *planting* system, but to open out new paths and to *diversify to the utmost extent our productions*.   This will secure immunity, to a great extent, against the accidents of the seasons, enlarge our markets, and bring into profitable employment much labor—as of women and children—now so little used.   And here permit me to remark that I regret to see that your committee, in making up their very large list of premiums, have failed to offer any inducements for essays or other information in regard to many—to us new—departments of industry.   A change in this respect is imperatively demanded by our altered circumstances.   In reflecting upon the many new fields of agricultural enterprise upon which our people might enter, I am forcibly impressed with the opinion that the two most promising of sure results, and best adapted to our scarcity of capital and labor, are the cultivation of the vine in the lowlands and the orchards and dairies of the highlands in these two States.   No surer road to fortune, it seems to me, can be found than lies here for intelligent industry.

The Scuppernong grape alone, with its various crossings, is a source of immense profit.   It is extremely hardy, its culture is simple, and since the clusters of Eschol, it is, perhaps, the most wonderfully prolific grape in the world.   Its home, too, is in that sandy belt covered by the long-leaf pine, heretofore erroneously considered almost valueless.

Here, without trenching at all upon valuable grain soils, enough wine could be made from it to supply the markets of the world, and place even in the cabins of the poor a purer and healthier drink than is now seen in the *salons* of the rich and great.

A statement of the yield and the sales of wine by a few gentlemen who have recently engaged in this business in North Carolina, would make many a man stare who continues to gather ten bushels of corn, or five of wheat, per acre, from his worn-out fields, after the manner of his fathers.

The capacity of this grape is indeed almost marvellous. I have derived some information in regard to the subject from a practical and experienced grower of it in Duplin county, North Carolina, which I give as follows: An acre will bear twenty-one vines forty feet apart. At three years old each vine yields one peck of grapes; at five, two bushels; at ten, twenty-five bushels; at fifteen, forty-five bushels; many vines actually bearing fifty bushels. A bushel of best grapes, weighing sixty pounds, will make four gallons of juice, which will yield about three and a half gallons of wine, readily commanding in market $2.50 per gallon. The pomice will make five gallons of vinegar, worth fifty cents per gallon. We have thus $11.25 as the proceeds of one bushel; $450 as the proceeds of one full-grown vine, $9,450 as the possible proceeds of one acre. A result that almost exceeds belief, and I state it with diffidence on what appears to me reliable authority. Even reducing every item by nine-tenths, it would still leave this grape the most prolific and most profitable one in the world; which I verily believe it to be. And I am assured by the best authority in the State that $1,000 per acre is a very moderate calculation. The labor and expenditures are very trifling, the whole not exceeding about thirty-three cents per gallon, including cost of real estate.

As to the wine itself, when properly made, Professor Charles T. Jackson, in the *Patent Office Report* of 1859, says of it: "The rich flavor of this grape renders it peculiarly valuable, the wine having the flavor and bouquet of the celebrated Tokay wine of Hungary. This grape, however, cannot be cultivated in the open air north of Virginia, and is a native of North Carolina. It is desirable that extensive vineyards should be established in that State expressly for the cultivation of this grape, which will make a wine that will be most eagerly sought for as the best of American native wines."

With regard to the difficulty existing in so calm a climate as ours of preventing the ascetic fermentation in the manufacture of wine, I suppose there need be no further trouble. I believe that is now pretty well established that although our summers are long, and the grape ripens while the season is yet too warm to make wine, the proper temperature can be obtained by means of vaults and cellars to secure the vinous fermentation in any part of the States; whilst in the frostless belts of the highlands the grape has been known to hang on to the vine in perfect keeping until December. This is, of course, the most favorable of all possible conditions for vine culture—a climate sufficiently warm to ripen the grape, and sufficiently cool at the season of the vintage to secure the vinous fermentation—sixty-five degrees being cool enough for that purpose.

A single fact is sufficient to show the capacity of this country for grape culture. The Scuppernong and the far-famed Catawba, the two best and most productive varieties on the continent, *are natives of North Carolina.* Strangers have transplanted them to no better soil and a far ruder and less congenial clime, and grown rich upon their culture, whilst we plough our worn-out corn-fields, hoe our soil-destroying tobacco, and talk of the hard times and the scarcity of money!

The mountains of this country present an appearance rather different from the general order of nature. The greatest elevations in America east of the Rocky Mountains are found in Western North Carolina, which Professor Gizot calls the culmination of the Appalachian system.

Unlike most mountainous regions, there is here no barrenness. They are clothed with timber to the very topmost ridge, and seven-tenths of their surface displays a soil of wonderful fertility, generally increasing in richness as you go up. Settlements were of course first made in the valleys and on the lower slopes, and the high mountain sides were supposed worthless, except for the wild pasturage furnished by the pea vine and the indigenous grasses. The forest growth of their rich coves and inaccessible ravines, consisting in part of every variety of oak, walnut, wild cherry, white pine, hemlock and mahogany, is perhaps unsurpassed in value and magnificence in the United States. Recently, however, a few enterprising citizens there are demonstrating by experiment that these fertile mountains are really our richest treasures. They are found to be invaluable for the production of grass, whilst corn, oats, rye, potatoes, and all other crops requiring coolness and moisture, flourish with a most remarkable exemption from either frost or drought. An experiment was tried there recently which is eminently worthy of mention. A high mountain ridge within six miles of the town of Asheville, in Buncombe county, N. C., was purchased for about one dollar per acre; 1,000 acres fenced in; along the crest of the ridge the undergrowth was cut down, and the trees deadened, in midsummer, no mattock being used. When perfectly dry, the whole was swept by fire, and the grass seed scattered without the plough. In riding over it in July, 1867, I found much timothy and orchard grass full six feet high. This year a cheese factory has been established upon it with every assurance of success, and besides grazing 150 cows, it fattened for the Southern market nearly 300 head of beef cattle—about 1,200 acres being in grass. This pioneer movement will be speedily followed up by many similar ones.

To show our people what profits may be derived from dairy farming—to most of whom I apprehend it is new—I will state a few facts in regard to this cheese factory as I learned them last summer. A gentleman, who is largely interested in the enterprise, sold four cows to the company at an average price of $21 each on a credit of six months. They proved to be fine milkers, yielding for nearly six months of the cheese making season about four gallons each per day. Each gallon of milk made one pound of cheese, worth twenty cents at the factory. So that before the day of payment each cow had paid $146—at least $100 of which was net—in addition to the calf and to the whey fed to the pigs. It is true this was an exceptional case, the great majority of the cows not yielding near so much, but it shows what *can* be done with good cows and good pasturage on land that cost originally one dollar per acre.

Again, a young farmer living near by, who milked fourteen cows—very ordinary, and from a pasture not at all fine—by sending his milk to the factory and exchanging it, a gallon of milk for a pound of cheese, made from that source alone about $750 in the season clear money—more than from all his farm besides! These facts are highly suggestive.

Literally, hundreds of thousands of acres of these rich and fruitful highlands—pastures of the sky—await the hand of enterprise in the bosom of our Southern Alps.

Of the fruit grown there—especially the apples—I confidently affirm there is not their equal in the United States either in quantity or quality. Eighty bushels are not unfrequently gathered from one tree, and in size and flavor I have never met with any in the markets of our Northern cities to equal them. This under a very poor and unscientific system of cultivation. Says Professor Kerr: "There is probably no better region for fruit in the United States. Apples grow almost spontaneously, and there are many seedling va-

which have originated here that are equal to the most cele-
exotics. And I have seen apples of good quality growing
n the tops of the mountains, nearly five thousand feet high,
the seed had, probably, been accidentally dropped by the
r."

the bosoms of these highlands is also observed a phenomenon
e curious and suggestive of most important results. Exten-
ones are found in certain localities, and at certain elevations
t entirely exempt from frost or dew. These frostless reaches,
sometimes, though scarce properly, isothermal belts, are be-
g well known and appreciated there. Professor Kerr suggests
llowing theory in regard to this phenomenon, but premises by
he had never yet investigated for himself, and says he does
ve it with confidence. "This phenomenon of frost, limited to
ain horizontal line along the mountain slopes, is of course
vitnessed in calm weather. In such circumstances the atmos-
arrange themselves in horizontal layers according to their
nt specific gravities, just as in elastic fluids, water and alco-
water and spirits of turpentine. The fact is rendered patent
eye by the horizontal smoke strata which you have seen in a
evening at sunset arranging themselves along the hills, or fog
in Buncombe. Now, each of these belts has its own pecu-
s of constitution—specific gravity, *humidity and tempera-*
-diminishing upwards. The deposition of moisture from any
se zones in the form of frost (or dew) will occur as soon as the
rature of the soil is reduced by radiation to the dew point,
of course, is always a point of temperature *below that of the*
elf. Supposing the radiation (and rate of reduction of the
ature of the soil) to be sensibly equal at different elevations,
ain that the dew point will be reached in these different strata
osphere successively from below upwards, and for any given
on may not be reached at all during the whole night. Ac-
ly, you may hear of such frostless regions in any of our
in counties, the belt being generally narrow, varying from
ods to several hundred yards in width, extending often quite
the sides of a cove or valley enclosed between mountain
The elevation of the lower limit of such zones above the
is said to vary very little for any given locality. As far as
rmation goes, it is generally from five or six hundred to a
id feet."

the delicate fruits—as the peach, the grape, and, I imagine,
r—can be grown with absolute certainty. I have stood my-

self and gazed with wondering admiration over the lovely valley of
the Swannanoa, the prettiest daughter of Mt. Mitchell, at the effect
of a hard spring frost upon the half-opened vegetation. Up to a
certain line in the mountain sides, drawn with the accuracy of the
spirit-level, the tender leaves were black and frost-charred, whilst
all above were still green and untouched! Such are Nature's efforts
to teach her children her hidden mysteries. It was her voice
crying out, "Plant here, plant here, and thy fruits shall never
fail."

Having premised by referring only to the dairies and orchards of
the mountains as a new and profitable source of enterprise, I shall
say nothing of their adaptation to other productions, to manufac-
tures, of their mineral wealth, the progress of railroads, or of their
scenery and healthfulness; and if I have said more in regard to the
resources of the mountain regions of my own State than of Virginia,
it is only because I know them better. I doubt not but that the two
regions are very similar, and that hints in regard to the one may be
equally applicable to the other.

In regard to labor, I don't permit myself to doubt but that the
candid historian will be compelled to say that in the existence of
Southern slavery the slaves were vastly more benefitted than their
masters. In a hundred ways it was a drawback upon our material
prosperity. It drove all the immigration to the North, and that
tide, of which we should have received a share but for slavery, has
made the free North rich and great. Fully conscious of this, as
Southern statesmen have ever been, they resisted abolition, not because they doubted the superiority of the free *white* labor, but
because they knew the utter worthlessness of free *black* labor.
They believe, and truly, that as this population was *here* it would
retard our prosperity *less* in a state of slavery. Here is the true
cause of our present condition. With slave labor in our midst there
was little or no room for European immigration, which could not
compete with it. *Now*, that the foreign labor can compete with the
negro, political causes of still greater weight interpose to prevent
his coming. The negro, for whom there is well-known repugnance
in all classes of European society, is not only still here, but he is,
under our present anomalous state of things, the master of the situ-
ation. It will be next to impossible to get any considerable quantity
of intelligent immigrants to cast their fortunes in a land cursed with
the African domination. The first duty of the agriculturist, then,
is a political one—to remedy this evil and secure a stable government, controlled by intelligence and property. I have confidence

that this will soon be done. · It is a law of nature that the superior shall govern the inferior.   Knowledge *is* power.! and not all the acts of Congress supported by all the bayonets within the power of insane men to apply can long succeed in reversing the decrees of God, and keeping Congo and Dahomey on top of Virginia and North Carolina.   When our political relations are properly adjusted—and not till then—may we expect an influx of white labor. Nor *even then* need we expect it unless we can offer it inducements. What can we offer it *now?*   What have we to pay?   In what department of agriculture do we hold out promises of profitable labor.?—enough so to direct immigrants from the rich, cheap lands of the great West?   I am decidedly of the opinion that we shall not be wise in either bringing or attempting to bring Europeans here to raise cotton or tobacco.   I feel well assured such a thing would fail.   The true character of the labor we should seek for is that which will enable us to *diversify our productions and develop new sources of wealth—open new fields of enterprise.*   We need herdsmen and cheese makers from the Alps, shepherds from the Scotch highlands, vine-dressers from the Rhine and the Pyrennes, hop-growers from Kent and Herfordshire.   Will such come upon an experiment merely?   How many vineyards, how many cheese factories, sheep walks, and hop farms, have we in operation among us to which we can refer them as evidences of our country's capacity? We must make these experiments and establish the success of these enterprises ourselves, without which we might fail in making profitable the *hired* labor we should import, and we shall surely fail in getting here that *independent labor* of the farmer-immigrant, by far the most desirable.

But, with all these conditions accomplished, it remains for us to consider the best means for encountering the vast appliances and great inducements held out by the people of the Northwest, our rivals for this stream of European immigration, which annually seeks our shores.   Nineteen-twentieths of it, landing at New York, never sees the South, and never will.   It will travel westward in the same parallels of latitude, in obedience to well-known laws, aided and encouraged by capital, speculation and organization, devoted to this purpose.   Nothing can change this but direct trade with Europe from the South, and the establishment of lines of emigrant ships with ports not north of Norfolk at least.   Then, with your aid societies, land companies, and similar organizations, a beginning could be made, which is all that will be required.   The success of the first colony will draw after it as much more as is desired. State aid to such an enterprise need not be expected as things are now constituted in the South—as the black element and black-white element which mingles with it are both deadly hostile to immigration. Nor is such aid essential or desirable. The railroad and municipal corporations of the South, aided by the great number of large land-holders, can raise ample means to put this great scheme into operation. I hope it will be done. The recent Commercial Convention in Norfolk was a move in the right direction. Still I would impress one thing: So great a change as this, from black to white labor, must be very gradually and gently accomplished, for various weighty reasons. There are many and great advantages in employing native labor, though it be inferior. The first instalment of foreigners are generally ugly customers, and until they learn us and we learn them we shall reap small profit from their superior industry and intelligence. It is plainly our duty, then, to make the very most of the native labor which we have. In many departments, I doubt not, the negro may be always valuable, and he is certainly our present dependence in our planting and staple growing operations. Then, too, political consequences must not be overlooked. Were it possible to fill the land with white immigrants to-morrow, it would not be desirable to convert the black population into paupers, vagabonds and criminals, by refusing to use their labor. Whilst I repeat my opinion that free black labor is a failure, and will never compete with the white successfully, yet it *is here,* and will *be here long,* and while here we should *use it at its worth,* subordinated to the other. Sound economy demands this of us, the peace and good order of society requires it, and humanity seconds the call.

And now, my countrymen and women, can I say anything more to help or encourage you in the promotion of your beneficent objects? Yours is the eldest born and noblest of human pursuits. All things in the world depend upon agriculture. The country blooms and prospers by it; civilization is its offspring; the great cities of the earth grow only by its help; the ships of the sea are but messengers of its bounty; and the roaring, smoking mechanisms of the world are the only factors of its wealth. The eloquence of the orator's tongue, the strength of the soldier's arms, the brightness of the poet's imagination, and the depth of the statesman's brain, the glory of the maiden's smile, the sweet music of lisping childhood—all, everything, comes from the worker in the earth! "Dust thou art, and unto dust thou shalt return," is the epitome of man's existence. "In the sweat of thy face thou shalt eat bread"—

the primal curse—it has become a blessing. God prosper you in your efforts to lift up and ennoble this great work—this guide and solace of human toil! I rejoice that its disciples are taking their true places among the honored ones of the world. I hope to see the day when the dull boy of the family will no longer be reserved for the farmer, and the brighter ones for the professions, so-called. The first work of man requires the best mind of man. The noblest labor should have the noblest talent. Tired of war, disgusted with its carnage, worn down with a civil strife worse than war, and sick at heart of all the triumphs and defeats of armed violence, when shall we learn to exalt the heroes of the victories of Peace?

VIRGINIA.—"Virginia," says Judge Sheffey in a recent charge to the Grand Jury of the Circuit Court of Rockbridge county, "is not without many blessings, although she stands under the shadow of a dark cloud of affliction. She is blessed with a population, white and colored, peaceable, orderly and submissive to law. She is blessed with resources unsurpassed by those of any State in the Union; her agricultural wealth, mineral products, water power, manufacturing capacities, climate, scenery and purity of atmosphere are unsurpassed. She is blessed with the cordial esteem and profound respect of civilized mankind; many of those who were once our enemies being foremost in applauding the unselfish devotion, calm dignity and stern heroism of her conduct during the recent war, and her patient submission and uncomplaining composure under sore trials and temptations since the war ceased, although peace came not; and she is blessed with that exalted self-respect which is better than wealth, better than bloated prosperity, better than well-fed complacency, and purse-proud self-laudation and boasting, and inspired with which her sons, even her colored people, when far from her borders, are wont to pronounce her name with proud confidence and with the assurance that honor awaits its whenever uttered; and above all, she is blessed in that she is yet standing, like the chief of the martyrs, with the sword of destruction suspended over her—still stayed and withheld by an invisible power; and as we gaze with fixed eyes and beating hearts at the venerable old State, and of so many other States, the framer of the Union and its fearless defender in years gone by, now bowed down and with her head bending forward to receive the blow which shall annihilate her as the old Commonwealth of Virginia, and as we see the uplifted arm stretched forth to destroy, still held back, may we not hope—at any rate, let us all fervently pray—that the 'arm which is not shortened' may yet save her from that doom which would make freemen mourn and patriots hang their heads in shame in the future!"—*Staunton Spectator.*

Horticultural Department.

Horticultural Literature.

With the increasing interest which is being aroused all over the State upon the subject of fruit culture, and to some extent a result of that interest, we have a mass of what may, for want of a more suitable term, be called horticultural literature. The columns of our daily, weekly and monthly press, secular and religious, teem with essays, communications, instructions, statements of profits, &c., until one is almost led to think that our whole people have become authors.

Ordinarily, there is little objection to be made to any, who feel an inclination and think they have the information to impart, giving said information to the public; for that which is valuable will be retained—the rest soon cast aside. But in the present circumstances, when the mass of our people are profoundly ignorant of the principles of fruit culture, yet feel the pressing need for embarking in it, as one of the surest and speediest methods of recuperating their wasted resources, it becomes a matter of the utmost importance that what they are told shall be reliable and practical. They are too poor to learn by the costly lesson of experience, that those who have undertaken to instruct know as little as themselves, in many instances less, and yet such must be their misfortune, unless something can be done to arrest the tide of exaggerated nonsense and, in many cases, wilful misrepresentations which are flooding the press of the State from "so-called" horticultural writers. We would not speak harshly of any, nor for a moment discourage those who honestly tell what *they know* for the encouragement and profit of others; on the contrary, we heartily wish them success in their noble work. But it is against that class of penny-a-liners, whose ignorance is only equalled by their assumption, that we wish to warn our readers. Day by day we see most marvellous statements of profits, most positive directions for cultivation and dictatorial commands as to varieties to be planted, which are extremely amusing, or rather disgusting, to those at all familiar with the subject.

These noxious scribblers may be divided into two general classes. Those who, without any personal acquaintance with the subject, collect what others have said, and not having capacity to make proper allowances for season, climate, soil and other circumstances, publish what mislead and deceive. Examples of this style are easily found. One of these authors reads somewhere that some one has made three thousand dollars from one acre in vineyard, and that fact (if fact it be) is immediately seized upon as a text from which to preach to our people, and they are told they can easily do the same. It is charitable to presume it to be through ignorance, not design, that the fact is conceded that such profits do not arise from the grape crop, but depend upon the sales of young vines propagated in the vineyard, and that it is only such vineyardists as are at the same time nurserymen that can expect any such truly marvellous returns. So with all other fruits. We are told that one thousand dollars per acre is a moderate income from strawberries, when in reality it is an extraordinary return, only to be obtained under exceedingly favorable circumstances.

Again, these writers deceive the public by their estimates and statements of capital and outlay required. Not less than five hundred dollars per acre will be required to prepare, plant and bring a vineyard into bearing, and yet we see those "who are too poor to own a mule and plough," advised that these are not essential, that all required is a pick and shovel in the hands of a man too poor to have his ground ploughed. But injurious as all this nonsense is, and deserving of censure as the authors of it undoubtedly are, still their condemnation is light compared with the withering contempt and disgrace which attaches itself to another class of these scribblers, viz: those who write with a view to advertising their own commodities. To-day, the unsuspecting reader revels in a most glowing description of some common-place varieties of grapes or strawberries, which, if he credits the half of it, must make him wish his whole plantation were covered with these plants, little thinking that the article is only meant to prepare the way for a long-winded advertisement of said varieties, to appear in the next days' issue. The consequence is he invests only to find, by experience, that he has wasted his substance for that which profiteth not.

How to counteract this growing evil is an important question, one, however, which the editors of the State can readily solve. Let them refuse to publish any commuuications, unless they know the authors to be not only reliable gentlemen, but also practically conversant with the subjects upon which they write. If this rule were adopted, we would have vastly less in quantity, and gain greatly in quality in the horticultural literature of the day. Our people want facts, not theories; they want to know how this and that man have succeeded or failed here in Virginia; what were the circumstances attendant upon success or failure. It is of little value to them to know what suits Minnesota or Texas, or what some writer *thinks* is required here. They can think for themselves; what they need is proper data from which to draw conclusions.

The Excessive Evaporation Theory Again.

In an article in the *Gardener's Monthly*, Mr. Meehan, its editor, politely refers to our paper published in the *Southern Planter*, controverting his theory that plants are killed during cold weather by excessive evaporation.

He first states that we seem to differ from him *in toto;* and next comes to the conclusion that we virtually agree with him, and tacitly acquiesce in his evaporating theory. We are not willing to be made to assume such an absurd position. The editor of the *Gardener's Monthly* ought not to have given mere garbled extracts, which appear to fall in with his speculations, but which, if taken in connection with what precedes and follows, would show that our conclusions are founded upon facts and the laws which govern organized vegetable life; and that these phenomena and laws are utterly at variance with the theory that evaporation is excessive in winter, and, consequently, plants die from want of proper nourishment. We reiterate what we have already stated, that during winter, especially in the Northern States, where the cold is severe, plants take in more moisture by capillary absorption carried on by means of the roots, in an unfrozen medium, perhaps, several feet below ground, than they give out by surface evaporation, brought about by the heat of the sun and the desiccating process of the winds.

While the absorption of moisture furnished by snows and rains which saturate the soil to a considerable depth is immense; the actual expenditures abstracted from plants is extremely insignificant. Evaporation can only become excessive in a hot and dry atmosphere when the vapor, instead of being condensed by cold, expands

ecomes lighter than air to make it ascend. Now, it is well
that these conditions do not exist during winter in Northern
es; nor can high winds produce evaporation in a direct way
cold weather. They have something of a desiccating effect,
se they carry off the vapor which is floating in the atmosphere,
one is ignorant of the fact that they do not dry muddy roads,
onsequently, do not evaporate the surplus water, but they only
the freezing process to go on more rapidly by suddenly ab-
ing the inherent caloric, and as soon as the weather becomes
, the roads become as muddy as ever.

other fact, which is no less indisputable, militates much against
Meehan's theory of excessive evaporation. During the winter
rganic system of plants, like that of some animals, becomes
to a great degree. Living organisms must be nourished from
it, because they are continually growing or enlarging their
nd perfecting their organization; they are producing new in-
als or germs of individuals which requires a constant supply of
materials. In cold climates, plants produce nothing during win-
nd, consequently, in this state of comparative inaction, the
ation of the organic fluids is extremely slow, just enough to
them alive and to maintain, so to say, their *status quo*. While
not deny that they evaporate some little moisture during dry,
weather, and therefore lose slightly by waste, we do emphati-
deny that "they give out more than they take in," and, con-
atly, die from inanition, as the doctors call it; and we as
tically assert that instead of starving from want of liquid
ials to nourish them, they have always a superabundance at
command, and might consider themselves, like some inveterate
, as "being drowned in wine and frolic."

, therefore, hold fast to our first position, that plants die dur-
cessive cold weather on account of the sudden abstraction of
vital heat, which is as necessary to their organic existence as
the higher animals. If Mr. Meehan will only visit his hot-
during winter, he cannot fail to observe that most of his
s flourish only in a warm temperature, which must be artifi-
provided, otherwise his plants would wither and perish; not
e their nourishment has been withheld, but because they were
pplied with a sufficient quantity of heat.

is it strictly true, as Mr. Meehan seems to intimate, that "by
re only does heat circulate through a plant, and it is only by
ation a circulation of heat is kept up, with evaporation heat
s." If Mr. Meehan means that plants cannot live without

sap or circulating fluid, we agree with him.   If it is his opinion that vital heat is one of the elements of plants indispensable to sustain their vitality, and that a circulating fluid is necessary to generate it and distribute it, we are in full accord with him.   But we cannot subscribe to his doctrine—that moisture and heat are inseparable, and that the one is the inevitable concomitant of the other.   A plant may be saturated with moisture, and still it may die by the sudden abstraction of heat, without the least evaporation having taken place.   Blossoms and buds are killed during cold spring nights, when no evaporating process goes on.   A man who visits the regions of the North Pole does not die because his blood freezes or evaporates, nor does he die from want of nourishment, but he perishes on account of the sudden abstraction of vital heat, which benumbs his nerves, causes torpidity and puts a stop to the organic machinery.   The organism of plants is not as complicated as that of animals, but the same principles of vitality are applicable to both.   Animals cannot live without air and light, neither can plants. Animals must supply their waste, and must take in materials that foster their growth, so must plants.   Animals have an inherent vital power to resist, in some measure, external atmospheric influences; and long continued droughts, which dry up almost everything except vegetation, show that plants possess this power in a great degree.

Beyond this, plants as well as animals are subject to the ordinary laws of caloric, which has a tendency to establish an equilibrium, by withdrawing an excessive supply from one body and infusing it into another less impregnated with its subtle fluid.

It would be very unfortunate for mankind if this excessive evaporation theory were true; for during the summer, when the atmosphere is hot and dry, and the evaporating process is very active, while at the same time the supply of rain is often very limited, all plants would perish, and the earth would become uninhabitable.

A. Featherman.

The Catawba Grape in Virginia.

"Blest is the country," exclaims William Cobbett, "that can grow Indian corn!"   "Blest the region," cries the Northern grape culturist, "that will ripen the Catawba!"   The host of new grapes invented in that enterprising section are but so many ineffectual protests against the forbidding climate that excludes that noble variety.   It forms the standard of excellence for the table and for wine. The Cedar Point Catawbas are the dessert fruit of the million in New York, and Catawba cobblers are the delight of the bibulous. Who ever heard of a Hartford Prolific cobbler or an Iona cobbler?

The few famed nooks north of Harrisburg, where this queen of American grapes is at home, have profited as the abodes of royalty usually do. They are all in the immediate vicinity of large bodies of water. Beginning west, we find such spots along the eastern shore of Lake Michigan, not more than two or three miles distant. Kelley's Island, in Lake Erie near Sandusky, has been famous in this respect for ten or fifteen years. The desired conditions reappear on the lake sides of Western New York. In these localities, land has risen from fifteen or twenty to eight hundred dollars an acre since their capacity for producing the Catawba was discovered. The other varieties grow and bear well enough in nearly every part of the North not beyond Albany. But only in a few such spots as we have named, and others on the promonitories of the Hudson below the Highlands, have such results been seen in the enhanced value of land.

Now, in the Piedmont and Valley counties of Virginia, no grape thrives better than the Catawba. It is our conviction that it will succeed quite as well in the Falls region, as we may call that along the head of Tide-water, if due attention be paid to the choice of situations and soils. On flat fields, more or less wet, surrounded by a belt of woods and having little or no trace of lime or potash, it can not be expected to do well. It needs a free circulation of air and a dry and strong soil. It will do where tobacco will. We have eaten as fine Catawbas in Charlotte county as we recollect anywhere. In precisely such a country it had its origin.

While the Concord is a fine grape, it has never held its own in the market against the Catawba. Those sections, however, where the latter has failed after a fair test, cannot do better than grow the former for the table and for general market purposes. It ripens earlier here than at the North, and seems to be quite as vigorous and prolific.

But Virginia has another string to her bow. The Norton is the specialty of those portions of the eastern territory where the Catawba fails. Its wine ranks first, and it cannot be depended on at the North. These two will always give her vineyards the advantage. They are both of wild origin, and it is not likely that any of the garden seedlings which crowd Northern catalogues, in ever lengthening lists, will ever equal them for the table and the cellar.

Finer varieties may in time be discovered or originated at the South, but they will not enure to the benefit of Northern growers, or interfere with Virginia's command of the Northern market. The Scuppernong, so admirable for wine, does not seem to make headway as a table grape in the Eastern cities, owing in part to its unattractive appearance. It, like the Catawba, is a wild grape from the Carolina woods. The same unexplored wilds may furnish the connecting link—a pulpless Catawba and a Scuppernong in bunches. Or, why may not some Southern experimentist follow the footsteps of the Allens and Rogerses, of Massachusetts, and operating on better material than theirs, produce the hybrid the country is waiting for?

But we are wandering from our original idea, which was to show that nine acres out of every ten in Virginia can, and ought to, yield a grape which not one acre in fifty thousand at the North can grow or will ever grow.   B.

Gardening in Arkansas.

Mr. Editor,—Two things are absolutely necessary for a good garden—a genial climate and a generous soil—and these essentials Arkansas possesses to an extent, perhaps, unequalled by any of our Southern States.

The almost annual overflow of the Mississippi imparts to the soil a richness equal to the valley of Nile, and then when you are told that a rock is something unheard of in this fertile and well watered land, you readily perceive that nature, both positively and negatively, has more than done her part, and he who suffers for " the staff of life " in this country richly deserves it.

Believing there is far more dignity and manliness in manual labor than in lounging about store-doors, whittling sticks and chewing tobacco, immediately on my arrival and settlement there I took hold of my garden with " my own hands," in true apostolic manner, and you know when I take hold it is rather hard to make me let go.

Tomatoes, cabbage, beets, onions, salsify, &c., were immediately transplanted from other hands, as it was too late to sow the seed; from these the yield has been abundant, and that, too, at no cost but about an hour's work by myself every morning.

Cymlings, snaps, water and musk-melons were then planted, and just now we have more than we know what to do with.

The Irish potato, a sort of hobby with me in my old Virginia garden, was planted after the same fashion—hills three feet apart, two to three cuts in a hill.   I did not get them in, however, till 1st of June.   They are now yielding finely. . The seed cost $2 (now dull at fifty cents) a bushel, brought down the Mississippi by those floating curses of this beautiful country—flat-bottom boats from Indianna and Illinois—which drain this poor people of every dollar they can rake and scrape, and then laugh in their sleeves at their stupidity and improvidence.

Digressing a little, I had a nice pan of egg-bread for breakfast this morning, made of Arkansas meal (new), the first I have eaten since I came out, which cost me fifty cents a bushel.   The same meal, kiln-dried in Illinois and as tasteless as saw-dust, held in our stores at $1.50.   (Do you think it possible for a man to starve in this country?)

Corn will not bring over $1.50 a barrel here this fall.

This leads me back to my garden.   The first of July I planted a large portion of it alternately in corn and peas, and am now feasting and fattening on them.   I wish you would send me by express this fall a quart of old-fashioned black-eyed corn-field peas.   We can't get the genuine out here, and are compelled to plant what is called the stock pea, which runs all over the face of the earth.

The sweet potato grows here to perfection, the alluvial soil making it yield most enormously.   I shall have an abundance of them in a few weeks.   They are dull in our market at $1 per bushel. . They are generally planted in beds, though I greatly prefer the hill.   They can be raised as readily from a cut from the vine as the hot-bed, as the dampness of the climate in the early spring makes them grow off very readily.

Though it looks late to the Virginians, yet I have been sowing winter cabbage seed, turnips, and planting snaps to-day (second crop).

We really have no winter to any extent before Christmas, and then rains supply the place of snow in our more northern latitudes.

One word more, and I have done this hurried letter.

Try and impress upon our people the necessity of saving their own garden seed instead of buying them from our Northern gardeners.   Hundreds of dollars go North annually from our poor stricken people for these simple little things, when a few moments attention daily would save this amount which might so much better be bestowed upon the education of our dear children ; but "Ephraim is joined to idols," and sometimes we are disposed to let him alone. Burning the child to the very quick does not seem to make him dread the painful element in the least.

In my next, I shall perhaps have somewhat to say about *making tobacco in Arkansas.* Would our people believe me if I were to tell them I have seen it high enough to hide a mule?

Yours, &c.,

THOS. WARD WHITE.

Helena, Arkansas, September 3d, 1868.

P. S.—I have been tempted these hard times to buy some of our soil and send it back to Virginia to be substituted in place of the thousand and one phosphates and super-phosphates which take all the money out of the country and leave nothing behind.

A little boy asked my wife the other day what sort of a thing was *manure,* and what did they do with it where she came from?

FALL TREE PLANTING.—The earlier in autumn that tree planting is performed the better, provided the wood has matured. It is not requisite that the leaf has fallen; but in transplanting, the leaf should be removed ere the tree is dug from the ground; keep the roots from drying cold winds or clear hot suns, and when setting spread them out regularly, and see that fine earth is next against each and every fibre; for where one root is laid against another without soil intervening, it is liable to dry and decay, and often destroy the whole tree. Do not pour water in among the roots at this time of year, but press and mingle the earth carefully with the hand and spreading fingers. Mound up around the tree about eight inches high, to assist it in retaining its upright position and also to carry off surplus water, for no matter how carefully the tree be planted, if water is permitted to stand around it and soak the roots from day to day, it may be expected to die.—*Horticulturist.*

With us the wood is now mature, and trees should be planted as soon as possible.—ED. SOUTHERN PLANTER AND FARMER.

STRAWBERRY BEDS planted this autumn should during this month be lightly mulched with coarse straw, cornstalks, or other litter that will serve to shield them from sun and prevent the ground from freezing and thawing rapidly; but at the same time the mulch should not pack down on the plants to smother them.—*Horticulturist.*

"Every man, in his prosperity, should make provisions to meet adversity."

Household Department.

Barn-Yard Poultry.

Domestic fowls are as subject to diseases as human beings; and some of their diseases are not unlike those that attend frail humanity "from the cradle to the grave." "Consumption" in man, and "Roup" in fowls are not dissimilar, in many respects. Man often inherits this disease from his parents. The chicken inherits "Roup" from his parents. Both suffer with coughs—with loss of appetite—with difficult breathing—with wasted strength—with loss of flesh—and if, perchance, skilful treatment and good nursing apparently restore them, slight exposure to damp night air, excessive fatigue, or improper diet, may cause the disease to return in a more aggravated form than it originally assumed. "Croup," in children, is said to be similar in its nature to "Gapes" in fowls. "Dyspepsia" in man, and "Hard Crop" in chickens, are but disorders of the digestive organs. Cholera and Apoplexy are common to man and fowls; and originating in like causes, require similar treatment.

"ROUP"

is the most fatal of all diseases to poultry, and the most difficult to master, when once it gets fairly seated in the poultry-yard, that I know of, and I doubt if there is any certain cure for it. Time and again have I nursed a few "roupy fowls" as if they were children, hoping to see them restored to health—and in some instances I have had them to rally and seem to be getting well; but the first cold spell brought a return of the disease, and after a few days' suffering, death generally relieved them.

Many causes have been assigned for "Roup," and many *specifics* published for its cure, but I have yet seen none that I deem reliable. Feeding liberally on stale bread soaked in ale, giving iron and assafœtida in their drinking water, and keeping the "Roupy fowls" in a comfortable room, will often palliate the disease, but its seeds remain, to be developed on the first suitable occasion. The safest plan is to kill or remove the sick birds as soon as the disease is discovered, and thus prevent the spread of the contagion.

"GAPES."

"Gapes" is a common, and often fatal, disease, sometimes taking off entire broods in the course of a few days. I have never seen a chicken with "Gapes" that was not full of *vermin.* My treatment is, to anoint the bird well with a composition made of tobacco and sassafras root bark, stewed in lard. This readily destroys all intruders. I then give the patient alum water and a drop or two of spirits of turpentine, and repeating the dose for a few mornings, soon find the little sufferer entirely recovered. An intelligent medical friend, who has made a careful diagnosis of "Gapes," pronounces it similar to *croup* in children, and recommends the same treatment for both.

"CHOLERA."

"Cholera" or "diarrhœa, if taken in time, will readily yield to chalk and cayenne pepper, mixed in the food of the sufferers. When they refuse to eat it, confine them till they are hungry, and then feed them moderately on the prepared dough.

Poultry sometimes die of apoplexy. Within twelve months, I have lost two fine hens by that disease. Bleeding might have saved them, had they survived long enough for the lancet to be used.

Weak joints, gout, etc., may be treated as diseases by some. Having no use for that class of "birds," I generally dispose of them in a more summary way.

I have hurriedly noticed some of the diseases to which poultry is subjected, and have recommended such remedies as I have found efficacious. That they will generally give satisfaction to those who take proper care of their poultry, I am quite sure; but to those who fail to feed their birds regularly—to give them pure air, fresh water and comfortable quarters, and to keep them free of vermin, no medicine will save them from pestilential diseases and death. Cleanliness is essential to the health of fowls, and he who undertakes to rear poultry without it undertakes a hopeless task.

BREEDS TO RAISE FROM.

The "White-Faced Black Spanish" is by far the best layer I have ever seen—but the young are the most difficult to rear. Not only are they subject to "Roup," "Gapes" and other diseases, but they breed more vermin, and suffer more from them, than the common "Dunghill" or any other "strain" of birds that I know of. I am making an effort to cross this breed in the imported Brahma, but cannot now say how the cross will succeed.

The "Brahma" is, perhaps, the best breed for our climate, and is said to succeed well at the North. They are good layers, sit well, and make good mothers. Their eggs are very large, and the young birds are ready to eat at eight or ten weeks old. Where they are free from "Roup" they are industrious and amiable; but the difficulty with us is to get them pure and, at the same time, healthy. I have now a letter before me, from a reliable gentleman in New York, of whom I ordered a few pairs, some weeks since, who says he attended the New England Poultry Fair, and could not fill my order, because *every chicken* on exhibition was diseased— *none of them* being worthy a premium.

CROSSING.

The Brahma and the Irish Gray (game) fowl will doubtless make an admirable cross for the table; and, it may be that the "Creve-cour" and "La Fleshe" (French importations) will make fine layers for this section; but until they can be procured of reliable dealers— men who have some regard for their reputations, and will not ship you diseased fowls—it were better to improve our present stock, by judicious crossing and careful breeding.

In conclusion, let me impress upon your readers the necessity of cleanliness, the free use of lime, liberal feeding and fresh water, as essential to successful poultry raising. Without these, farmers cannot have that abundance of eggs and birds so essential to good living in country and town.

J. W. L.

"Sweet Pickle Cantaloupe."

Mr. Editor,—I suppose most of the readers of your excellent paper raise "citrons," or, as it is better known, cantaloupes, and I will give you an excellent recipe for putting them up for home consumption in the winter: Take one basket of cantaloupes, pare them and take out the seeds, and cut them in about six pieces, or better still, cut them through in every indentation; pack them in a large pan as close as possible; cover them with vinegar, and let them stand twenty-four hours; retain three quarts of the liquor, and to each quart allow three pounds of good light brown sugar, one ounce of cinnamon, and one half-once of cloves. Boil the syrup, at the same time skimming it, add the spice, and boil the melon twenty minutes; take out the pieces, and pour the syrup over them boiling hot; let stand until next day; then put the syrup on the fire, and when it boils, add the melons and boil the melons half an hour longer; put them in jars, and tie bladders over them. They are better six months or one year old. MRS. EVANS.

Town Point, Chesapeake City, Cecil county, Md.

THE SOUTHERN PLANTER AND FARMER.

RICHMOND, VIRGINIA, ... NOVEMBER, 1868.

TERMS OF SUBSCRIPTION AND ADVERTISING.

SUBSCRIPTION One Year,..$2.00

ADVERTISING.

1 square, 10 lines or less, one insertion,.....$ 1 00	¼ page, one year,...$ 35 00
1 square of 10 lines for six months,...... ...... 6 00	½ page, six months,...................................... 35 00
1 square of 10 lines for one year,.................. 10 00	½ page, one year, ... 60 00
1 page, single insertion,................................ 15 00	1 page six months,.. 60 00
¼ page, six months,...................................... 20 00	1 page, one year...100 00

PAYMENTS.

Subscriptions—in advance.   Advertising—annual—quarterly in advance.   All others in advance

Editorial Department.

Our Club Arrangements.

We furnish the following Journals at club rates:

The Richmond Christian Advocate (weekly), and So. P. & F., for $4 50 a year
The American Farmer, Baltimore, (monthly), and So. P. & F., for 3 50 a year
The Land We Love (monthly), and So. P. & F., for   .   .   4 35 a year
Moore's Rural New Yorker (weekly), and S. P. & F., for   .   3 75 a year
The Cultivator and Country Gentleman (weekly), and So. P. & F., for 3 75 a year

The Augusta County Fair and Speech of Commodore M. F. Maury.

All accounts concur in representing the Augusta County Fair as a complete success, reflecting the highest credit on the liberal and enlightened public spirit of the people of Augusta, and upon the President and Directors for the wise and judicious arrangements which they had made, under many disadvantages, for the success of the Fair and for the accommodation of the multitude of visitors.

We hope to give a full account in our next, but must be content, meanwhile, with appropriating all of our present available space to the reproduction of the admirable address of Commodore M. F. Maury, delivered on the second day of the exhibition as follows:

COMMODORE MAURY'S ADDRESS.

Fellow-Citizens,—I do not come here to make a speech, but to have a little plain talk with the Augusta farmers. We are told that you are wanting in energy, and lack enterprise. The spectacle before us does not look like it, especially when we consider the money and labor you have expended in the purchase and preparation of these grounds. That you lack energy is a mistake; I don't believe it. Error is always mischievous, and I think it best to correct the false impression. Apparently the North is more prosperous than the South, because the North is manufacturing and commercial, the South agricultural. In all manufacturing and commercial communities products are concentrated, and there is a show of life and activity which is never seen in agricultural communities, because labor is there diffused. Another reason is, that the statistics showing the rewards of labor at the North and South are not quite fairly presented. For instance, suppose that one of your neighbors, in giving you an account of his earnings during the year, should tell you that he had housed so many barrels of corn, which was worth five dollars a barrel; and killed so many hundred weight of pork, that was worth eight cents a pound; had so many pounds of bacon, worth twelve cents; but when you come to catechise him a little closer, you find that it had taken all of his corn to fatten his pork, and all of his pork to make his bacon.

Now, this is the way with the hay crop of the North, which they tell you is worth as much as the cotton crop of the South. In ths last returns, the hay crop of the North is put down at upwards of three hundred millions dollars; the value of the live stock at a little more, and the value of the butter and cheese at many millions, when the hay went to make it all. There is still another reason for this apparent greater prosperity of the North, and the apparent show of greater energy and enterprise there. According to the census of 1790, the population of the United States was very nearly equally divided between the North and South; and according to the returns of the subsequent census, the ratio of natural increase was greater at the South than at the North. But, notwithstanding this, the population of the North, according to the census of 1860, was, in round numbers, eleven millions greater than at the South.

Did it ever occur to you, when an emigrant comes into the country, to calculate how much he adds to the national wealth, not by the money which he brings, but by the labor which he is able to perform? For that labor you pay him, at the least, one hundred dollars a year. He, therefore, represents an industrial capital of which a hundred dollars a year is the interest, precisely in the same way that a steam engine, by the work which it is capable of performing, represents an industrial capital. The labor, therefore, of a white man represents quite as much industrial capital as the labor of a negro did before the war, which for an able-bodied man varied from twelve to fifteen hundred dollars. Taking old and young, male and female, let us suppose that each emigrant represents an industrial capital of four hundred dollars. And then we must take these eleven millions of excess of Northern population, as the number of emigrants, and the descendants of emigrants, which have come into the country since 1790 and settled at the North rather than at the South. Multiply that by four hundred and you have upwards of four thousand millions of dollars, which the North has acquired, not from any superior energy of her people, but merely by the influx of laborers and foreigners from abroad. Suppose these eleven millions had settled in Virginia, what would not have been the wealth of the State? So much for what transpired before the war. How is it since? The public prints and some public speakers are continually pointing to this and that source of wealth among us, and because it has not been more developed, charging us with a lack of enterprise.

I maintain that you—and in apostrophizing you, I mean the people of the South—I maintain that you, the farmers of Augusta, the country gentlemen of Virginia, the men of the South, have been and are applying your industrial energies with a degree of intelligence, skill, vigor and effect that is not excelled by any other people in the world. Man for man, your surplus products are not surpassed by any other people anywhere. This opinion may surprise some, but I maintain it, and to vindicate you I appeal to facts and figures, and to the official reports of the Government itself. There has been established at Washington a Bureau of Statistics. Mr. Delmar is the chief of that Bureau. He makes a report on commerce and navigation for 1867, and sends it to the Secretary of the Treasury. The Secretary of the Treasury forwards it to Congress for the information of the people, and my facts and figures are on this authority. The figures were obtained under oath, at least those of them which relate to the exports of domestic products, from which I am going to quote. These figures were obtained under oath from the ships before they were allowed to clear; and the statements thus made were tabulated in the various custom-houses, and transmitted to Washington, and it is from them that the statistician of the United States Government compiles his table, namely, a statement of the gross specie value of the exports of domestic products from the beginning of the Government to June 30th, 1867:

BUREAU OF STATISTICS— TABLE 18.

Statement of the gross specie value of exports of domestic produce from the beginning of the Government to June 30th, 1867:

[Extract in Millions.]

1857	.	.	. $338,000,000*	1863	.	. . $240,000,000
1858	.	.	. 293,000 000	1864	.	. . 241,000,000
1859	.	.	. 335,000,000	1865	.	. . 197,000,000‡
1860	.	.	. . 373,000,000	1866	.	. . 414,000,000
1861	.	.	. 382,000,000†	1867	.	. . 394,000,000
1862	.	.	. 213,000,000			

* The largest up to that year.

† War figures estimated.

‡ War figures.

Total exports of Southern products, during the fiscal year ending June 30th, 1867, currency value, (approximated) $328,400,759. Total exports of domestic products from the United States same year, currency value, $471,608,600.

Proportion of Southern products to all domestic products exported, 69 per cent.

Bushels of Indian corn, production of Southern States:

1859–'60.	1866–'7.
434,937,863.	320,605,513.

All the States.

838,792,740	867,946,295

Fifty-two per cent. by Southern States ante bellum.

Thirty-seven " " post bellum.

Population of the Southern States (U. S. census 1860) 10,259,017. Population of all the other States, 21,185,963.

Average bushels Indian corn in Southern States, 42½; in all others, 19—in 1860—(Estimate Bureau Statistics—Southern States, in 1866, 9,568,709 inhabitants; all the others, 24,916,765. Average bushels of corn to each person in Southern States, 33½; all the others, 22.

These are from the official documents of the Washington Government, and it is worthy of mark, that in assigning 69 per cent. of all the exports for the year ending June, 1867, to the Southern States, the Government statistician gives them no credit for breadstuffs, lumber, minerals, and the like, sent over the border. He estimates the population of the Southern States at 9,568,709; all the rest at 24,916,765, and makes the value of the domestic products exported by the former, $328,406,757; by the latter, $143,201,243; or he makes 28 per cent. of the population of the whole country to send abroad 69 per cent. of the total value of all its exports. In other words, notwithstanding the devastation of the war, the average domestic exports amount in value for each person in the Southern States to $34.32 per caput; in all the other States to $5.75.

He estimates the population of the South for the year ending June 30th, 1866, at 9,568,709, and of all the States together at 34,505,882. According to these tables, the South in 1866 had very nearly the population that the whole of the United States contained in 1820. And what were the exports of the domestic products of the whole country that year? Fifty-one million. The South in 1866 exported, according to the same authority, 272,000,000, specie value, more than five to one. In 1850 the population of the whole United States was, in round numbers, 23,000,000, and the domestic exports amounted that year to 136,000,000. The South now, with not the half of population of 23,000,000, exported 272,000;000, being two for one.

But, notwithstanding these facts, opinions have got abroad most injurious to the South, and which it is essential to correct. Mr. Adams, a few days ago, in his speech at Charleston, tells us what Massachusetts thinks of the Southern people; that the traditional idea of a Southern man there is a dirk in one pocket, and pistol in the other; a cigar in one side of his mouth, and a quid of tobacco in the other; indolent and domineering and intolerant of any difference of opinion. A Northern gentleman who had established himself in South Carolina, in discovering what a goodly land it is, and how peaceably disposed are the people, writes to his friends thus:

"I had been led to believe that it was dangerous for a Northern man to travel here, and that robberies and outrages were common. It would naturally be supposed that the officers of the Freedmen's Bureau were peculiarly obnoxious to Southerners. Yet I find that Major Stone, the assistant commissioner of this district, traverses the country not only without a guard, but even a pistol to defend himself from attack, and Major Walker, the commandant of the post, states that in his opinion life and property is as secure here as in any of the Northern States. Now the town of Aiken is partly in Edgecombe and partly in Barnwell district, than which none were more thoroughly secession. This winter and spring hundreds of Northern persons, of all shades and grades of public opinion, have visited this town, and I have yet to hear of the first one who has been molested or insulted.

"The physical characteristics of this section are very different from our preconceived notions. The phrase 'down South' raises a picture in many minds of dense swamps, umbrageous woods, tropical plants, sluggish streams, venomous reptiles, yellow fever and miasma. How much this idea is due to pictures usually found in school books, I will not stop to inquire."

The North, entertaining these opinions of us, did not fail to impress the European mind with them. Accordingly you hear Vernon Harcourt, one of the rising men of England (who was the author of the celebrated papers written during the war over the signature of Historicus, upon the rights of belligerents and the duties of neutrals) say the other day before the Social Science Congress at Manchester, at which all the European world was present, that "Gentlemen who had travelled in the Southern States have often seen persons sit down to a peaceful dinner with a revolver in each coat-tail pocket. Of course it was only for the purpose of self-defence, but then it very frequently happened that before dinner was over two or three were shot." I doubt whether there is a gentleman present here in this vast assemblage with a pistol in his coat-tail pocket.

But we are to expect another slander. We are to expect to hear it said on this side of the water that this large amount of surplus products annually sent abroad from the South is owing to the labor of freedmen. But gentlemen who assert this, forget that in turning loose from the field 4,000 000 blacks, they put into it 6,000,000 whites. Now, how came it, let us ask, that the impression that the South was lacking in energy and wanted enterprise got abroad? I will tell you how it came to pass. Gentlemen from New England came here who could understand and appreciate the value of our water power, but who knew nothing about the agricultural resources of our State; and they, therefore, said to themselves, very naturally, what would not this water power, which is running to waste be worth, if utilized? Would it not be worth more than all the coal and iron of Pennsylvania? And because we did not utilize it to its full extent, it was taken as a proof that we were indolent and idle. Again, a gentleman from the mining districts of England would visit us now and then, and he would see and appreciate the vast mineral resources that lie undisturbed in their veins and hidden in the mountains, and would tell the fabulous sums that these would be worth in England. And because they were not utilized, he would say that we lacked energy. But we knew that agriculture was more profitable than they, and we devoted our energies and enterprise to agriculture as the most remunerating industry.

This water power that is running to waste, and these minerals that are lying idle, are our "tailings." It is very profitable sometimes, as you all know, to work ,' tailings;" and we now want labor from abroad—labor that is skilled in manufacture and in mining, to help us to also turn to account these sources of wealth. But as for ourselves, our land is so teeming with the benignant bounties of nature, that we have not the force or the time to attend to these other great sources of wealth.

Did you ever reflect that Virginia is in the latitude of the promised land; that the same skies upon which David and Solomon and our Saviour gazed, are garnished for us as they were for them; that the Pleiades, Orion and Arcturus rise and set, and shine upon us as they did upon Job; and that everything that is grown there, from the fig and the vine, the corn and oil, grow here as well—and other things besides? Did you know that Virginia and North Carolina have given the greatest gifts from the vegetable kingdom that have been given to man since history began?—that the Indian corn, the potato and tobacco, besides other things, were gifts from this part of the world? Does it show any lack of enterprise or of energy to turn such bounties as these to account, and to teach the world their value?

Talk of enterprise and daring! Who was it but the sons of Virginia and North Carolina who first crossed the Alleghanies and drove the Indian and the wild beast? and in doing so they encountered dangers, hardships and sufferings to which those of the Pilgrim Fathers bear no resemblance; and after they went, it was then, that the enterprising Yankee followed.

Let no man hereafter reproach you with a want of what he calls a little Yankee enterprise. We don't want it. What we do want is Yankee thews and sinews—the hard-fisted immigrant, the man of means; a little of the industry and good husbandry for which the Dutch and the Danes and the Germans are so famous, inspired and inspirited by a little Southern enterprise and energy. That's what we want. Give us that, and we will show you upon the hills and in the valleys of our dear old Virginia such an abode of human happiness and prosperity as the world never saw.

But how are we to get these emigrants? The Virginia Military Institute has undertaken to make known the great natural resources of the State. But after it shall have published its account of them, how shall we get it to the ears of those abroad who wish to know the truth about us? We have no means of circulating it there. Southern papers and Southern periodicals are read only by the few, and they a very few, in Europe. We want the million to learn of these good things, and I can think of no better means of doing it, than that the farmers of Virginia exhibit a degree of public spirit similar to that which the farmers of Augusta have done with regard to this Fair; and by raising a fund for the translation of these reports into the German and other languages of Europe, and for circulating them there extensively.

And that these reports shall convey the information most desirable and most useful to the emigrant, it is very much to be desired that the farmer shall furnish answers to the questions which have been propounded to them from the office of the Physical Survey of the Institute. The Dutch are already alive to the importance of this subject, and are talking of a line of steamers from Flushing to Norfolk. Holland is situated with regard to the centre of Europe and the sea-shore, as Virginia is. At Flushing, Holland affords the nearest and best seaport to all of Southern and Central Germany, extending as far back as the Valley of the Danube; precisely as the Tide-water harbors of Virginia do the nearest seaport to the centre of the Mississippi Valley, to St. Louis, and all the landings on the Missouri river. Virginia furnishes the ports which are farthest to the North, that are never obstructed by ice in winter. The same with Flushing on the other side. Flushing is but five hours' steaming from England. Flushing and Norfolk are between Baltimore and Bremen, where there is already a line of steamers in successful operation. The Dutch Government, appreciating at last the importance of Flushing as a seaport town for the heart of Europe, is now extending her lines of internal improvement from Flushing into her back country. This is what Virginia is seeking to do. Our Dutch friends say, "Give us a second, and we will bridge the Atlantic with a line of boats between Flushing and Norfolk!"

There is, I think, one thing which the farmers of Virginia have to learn, and that is to act more in concert than they have been doing. In travelling through the old countries you will observe that the farmers have there learned by experience that good roads are much more economical than bad ones. And if you, gentlemen of Augusta, could only visit France and England and see the roads there and the loads that are drawn on them by one horse and one cart, I think you would come to the conclusion instantly that about the best thing you could do would be to club together and make good roads.

Another feature is very striking in those countries as to clubbing together and acting together. The Ameri an travelling there will be charmed with the highly improved country and its high state of cultivation—the elegant fields, the fine crops, and he will be continually looking for the splendid country mansions to which such fine plantations belong. But he will not find them. Although he will see many villages consisting of plain tenements, and which are the abodes of farm-hands, and he may find in the rural districts a village, perhaps as large as Staunton, in which I might doubt if he could find half a dozen houses in which meals are cooked. Suppose a village of a thousand houses, instead of having a thousand kitchen-fires and a thousand cooks daily at work for at least an hour or two, he will find two or three bake-houses, to which every family in the village sends its meat to be cooked. See what economy in fuel alone! It is the same with the bakery, and you will find emigrants coming here and wishing to settle, inquiring in the country, even, for the baker. These are small points, but in their multitude they involve vast sums.

Correspondence of Southern Planter and Farmer.

My Dear Sir,—In the running letters that I have lately addressed to you, some of our utilitarian philosophers will probably find little of practical value, yet I flatter myself that a majority of your readers will see in them something at least to excite serious reflection. I might, without difficulty, fill more than half your paper monthly with learned essays on the science of agriculture and its practical details, drawn from materials furnished by long study of the best authors, and more than forty years actual experience as a farmer. But of what avail would all this be to the great body of our suffering fellow-citizens? Who desires now to be informed upon the various theories of agriculture, or how to raise wheat, or corn, or peas, or beans, or potatoes, or turnips, or pumpkins, or squashes? It is not knowledge, but hope, that the people want. You know that I am of a most hopeful temper, and cultivate cheerfulness with as much zeal as others do cabbages and ruta-bagas, yet I cannot close my eyes or ears to the signs of public distress, or be unmoved by the dark prospect before us. The last crop of wheat barely paid expenses, and the corn crop of this year, taken as a whole from the mountains to the sea, is probably quite as short as any since the memorable season of 1816. The great breadth of land planted is urged as a reason in favor of an average crop, but this is one main cause of its failure. Large fields in the hands of freedmen unmanured and uncultivated, cannot yield a crop, especially of corn, which, of all plants, requires the most continuous and unremitting labor. The season was unpropitious, the spring rains and the summer droughts were alike disastrous, but the extensive failure may be assigned to the cause stated by your sensible correspondent from Granville, N. C., the want of the greatest of all fertilizers, "sweat," a healthy secretion which the Freedmen's Bureau seems to have dried up. Actual want is staring many in the face. A friend of mine, not twenty miles distant, said to me the other day, "there are three things very scarce in this neighborhood—*money, meat and bread.*" And I have no doubt if a searching inquiry were instituted, it would be found that these three wants are quite as urgent in other parts of the State.

In this state of destitution the people look forward with anything but hope to the new year. The STAY LAW will then expire by limitation, and the flood-gates of ruin will be opened upon them. My whole soul was in our late contest for public liberty. I perilled all, and was perfectly willing to lose all for success. The brave and generous, even among our enemies, will approve this sentiment, for they will know how to trust the faith of those who were true to what they believed to be the cause of the r country. I suffered in common with my fellow-citizens, and feel a melancholy satisfaction that I was deemed worthy to suffer in such a cause. I admire the sublime sentiment put by Addison into the mouth of Cato—it is not meet that Cato's house should escape the calamities of a civil war. I envy not the tranquility of those who, standing aloof, lost nothing by the contest, and now wrapping themselves securely in their warm doublets, safe from the storm, are regardless of the sufferings of those who must yield to its fury. Better far to have suffered with their countrymen, and to have become generous by misfortune, and to be able to re-echo the noble sentiment of Queen Dido—

Non ignara mali miseris succurrere dives.

I came out of the war with ten dollars in cash, with two broken down horses on farms of three thousand acres, with fields abandoned, flocks dispersed and lands, for the most part, desolate and uncultivated. I could not but feel the embarrassments common to our people, yet by a hopeful spirit and energy and perseverance, I have been able to keep the wolf from the door, and to avoid the entanglements of judgments and other liens, and I have reason to thank God that I and all my house, in all its branches, are relieved from the fear of want. But I love Virginia, her ancient traditions and true-hearted people, and I cannot contemplate without a pang the possibility of the utter ruin of so noble a race.

I am often asked by men, trembling with apprehension, "What is your opinion? Do you think the STAY LAW will be 'lifted' at the end of the year?" My invariable reply is, No! I cannot believe it possible that our people can be subject to so cruel a fate. Our military Governor is said to be a humane man, and can feel for the misfortunes of a brave people, and will know how to do his duty in his anomalous position. Now is the time for considerate judges, with the tact, judgment and mercy of the gentle Portia in the case between the Jew and the merchant of Venice, and for large-hearted legislators, whether civil or military, who can feel for the sufferings of the people, to do all in their power to mitigate their severity.

It is fashionable with the unfeeling or unthinking to denounce the STAY LAW as immoral in principle and ruinous in its effects. At the risk of my reputation for integrity, which has been maintained unimpaired through a long life of active intercourse with my fellowmen, I will maintain the opposite opinion. I approve the stay law. It was an imperative necessity, was just and expedient, and is to be condemned only, because it fell short of its great object in not suspending indefinitely the judgment lien, and thus cutting up by the roots the whole harvest of litigation. The State has failed (I grant from inability) to protect the property of her citizens, on the credit of which most of their debts were created, surely it cannot be unreasonable or unjust for the Government to stay the rigor of its civil remedies, until the people can have an opportunity of gathering up their scattered resources, and of making with their creditors the best settlement in their power?

There is a principle of natural justice of daily application in the courts of all maritime countries, which, if the Legislature had possessed the power, it might have applied with entire propriety, in the existing relations between creditor and debtor in this Commonwealth. When different persons ship in a common bottom, and a part of the cargo is thrown overboard to save the rest, all parties interested are required to contribute, on the principle of *general average*, to the loss which has been sustained for the benefit of all. This principle in the language of Judge Stay "is not the result of contract, but has its origin in the plain dictates of natural law." And the principle of justice may be regarded as of universal application, "that a loss sustained for the sake of all, shall be made good by the contributions of all." The people of Virginia engaged in the revolution or civil war for a common purpose, and almost with entire unanimity. We all entered upon a common venture, and were bound by natural justice to make equal sacrifices in the cause. The owners of slaves, of bank stock, of corporation and railroad stocks lost all, the holders of bonds and mortgages lost nothing. Why should these last not be required upon the principles of natural justice to contribute to the losses of their confederates? As the State has not the power to adjust these losses upon the principles of the court of equity, surely it cannot be wrong to stay the hands of the creditors, until the debtors shall have an opportunity to make available their property saved from the wreck, and to enter into such compromises as justice may demand? If for no other purpose, the stay law should be continued to encourage, if not to compel these compromises. If the stay law was a necessity at the close of the war, surely it is not less a necessity now. Our affairs, which were then in a hopeful condition, have been rendered, by subsequent events, almost desperate. Political agitation, the Freedman's Bureau, short crops and the want of the protecting and invigorating influence of a free State Government, have paralyzed the industry of the people. The act of the Legislature reviving the judgment lien after having for a short time suspended it, invited litigation, and nearly all existing obligations have been put in suit. The consequence is that more than half the homesteads of the farmers are encumbered with judgment liens. The act of Assembly (Code 771, § 9,) provides that these liens shall be enforced in the courts of equity, and whenever it shall appear that the rents and profits are insufficient to pay all the debts in five years, the land shall be sold. Let me illustrate the terrible effects of this provision. A thrifty farmer before the war owned a plantation worth $5,000, and slaves and other personal property worth $10 000. He has incurred debts for the improvement of his property amounting to $1,000. The war strips him of every thing but his land. He has not been improvident; he has committed no crime in contracting these debts. His creditors all sue him and obtain judgment. They summon him to a court of equity. The rental of his property administered by a court of chancery will not exceed 4 per cent, or two hundred dollars. The annual interest of the debt is sixty dollars, and to say nothing of the costs and charges of this expensive proceeding, the rents and profits will not pay the debts in five years, the lands must be sold, and the unhappy proprietor, with his family, be turned out of doors. This may seem to be an extreme case, but such cases will doubtless be frequent in the the general wreck of credit and property that must follow the repeal of the staw law. But what will be the effect upon the interests of creditors, when the debts are larger in proportion, and yet not so large that the property would not be sufficient under the prudent administration of the debtor, to pay the whole or a large part of the debts? Fees, costs, and commissions incident to the expensive proceedings of a court of equity would absorb the greater part of the scant proceeds of a forced sale, and the creditors, like parties in a suit in bankruptcy, would leave the court with small dividends and maledictions loud and deep on all concerned. How much better for both creditor and debtor to leave the debtor free to sell the whole or part of his property at a fair price, and pay his debts, or make such compromises with his creditors as may be deemed just.

It is believed by practical men who seem to be well informed on the subject, that the real property of the State, if sold at forced sales, would fall very far short of paying all the judgment and other liens upon it. Is it too much to ask that this cruel necessity may be avoided, which can be done only by continuing the stay law. But sixty days remain for action. Let creditors and debtors unite in a petition to the military commander of this district to interpose his authority to avert this dire calamity, by extending the stay law at least for another year.

I deem this subject at this time of far more importance to the farmers of Virginia than matters of practical agriculture, yet I do all in my power by precept and example to encourage them in their labors. I do not write on potatoes or turnips, yet I have a fair crop of potatoes, both sweet and Irish, and my crop of ruta-bagas though on a small scale, and manured entirely with home-made manures, is the best in all the country round about. My neighbors and friends, notwithstanding their many disappointments, are exerting themselves manfully to put in a wheat crop. My youngest son, after some interruptions from the weather, has put in, in the best style with his own hands with the drill, aided by a negro boy to fallow it, a fallow field of forty acres, and is now preparing, with such help as we may command, to put in a field of sixty acres of corn land, which I desire to put in grass. I mention these things to show that I by no means advise our suffering fellow-citizens to give way to despair, but to put their own shoulders vigorously to the wheel, though they may have to call on Hercules to help them.

Very truly, your friend,   WILLOUGHBY NEWTON.
Linden, Hague P. O., Westmoreland county, Oct. 9th, 1868.

Dear Sir,—I have had my last years' numbers of the *Planter and Farmer* bound for preservation. When packing them for the binder, I desired that the advertising sheets should be retained, as they will hereafter furnish a record of the machines, fertilizers, implements and classes of stock and seeds recommended by agricultural furnishers during the year—information which will surely be useful in future years. Owing to the fact that a different quality and *color* of paper is used for the advertising sheets, the book will be one of variegated colors. I would respectfully suggest that, if the difference of expense is not too great it might add to the value of your already very valuable monthly to have these useful sheets of the same color with the body of the magazine. Very respectfully,   CHAS. P. STONE.
Goochland county, October 17th, 1869.

In accordance with the suggestion of our correspondent, we have determined to use hereafter white paper in place of colored for our advertising sheet.—ED.

Mr. Editor,—I noticed in your September number of the *Southern Planter and Farmer* what you designate as "a new wonder," and I will describe a similar one that appeared on a Concord or Isabella vine last year. We had the pleasure of dissecting this fungus or excrescence, caused by some insect or poisonous fly. It appeared like a small apple about one inch from side to side, and one-half inch from stem to blossom end. The blossom end was very much sunken in; the eggs were deposited beneath the bark causing it to swell and assume the form of an apple. When opened, in the place the seeds ought to have been, if it had been a fruit, was occupied by small cells containing an insect about one-sixteenth of an inch long, and about as thick as a pin. Some of the cells contained a fly similar to the fly in the oak ball. I hope this will set at rest the theory, which I believe you and your readers had formed, that you had discovered a new fruit, or rather that an apple had grown on a grape vine. A few days ago we had the pleasure of dissecting another of the "new wonders," which was similar to the one above described.

Yours, very respectfully,

DAVID Z. EVANS, JR.

Town Point, Chesapeake City, Cecil county, Maryland.

Our Exchanges.

THE SEMINARY MAGAZINE—an illustrated Monthly—devoted to the interterets of education, and to the mental culture of the women of the South. Especial attention will be given to the Floral Department. Three or four handsome illustrations of the most choice flowers will appear in each number, with articles descriptive of each, mode of cultivation, floral interpretations, etc. Brief essays by school girls will appear in each number. Some of the best writers in the South will contribute to the Departments of Belles-Lettres, Light Literature, Natural History, &c. Each volume of twelve numbers will contain *seven hundred and sixty eight* pages of entertaining and instructive reading, printed in clear, distinct type, on beautiful white paper, with nearly one hundred handsome illustrations. Sixteen pages in each number devoted to the Sabbath School interest. Everything of a political or sectarian nature, or of immoral tendency, will be carefully excluded, and contributors are respectfully notified that articles of a sensational character will not be accepted. Subscription price $1 50 per annum, payable in advance. Address, M. W. Hazlewood, Box 961, Richmond, Va.

THE CAROLINA FARMER.—Monthly—32 pages octavo—price, $2 per annum. W. H. Bernard, editor and proprietor, Wilmington, N. C. It is gotten up with taste and liberality, and contains, in pleasing variety, a number of well written articles of an instructive and practical character, well adapted to the condition and wants of the Carolinas in particular and to the South generally. We wish it a prosperous and useful career, and welcome it as a co-laborer in the cause of agricultural progress and improvement.

CROMO LITHOGRAPHIC PORTRAIT.—We have received from L. Prang & Co., of Boston, a cromo-lithograph of "The Poultry of the World," containing "portraits of all known valuable breeds of fowls" to the number of fifty varieties. A splendid specimen of this new achievement in the fine arts. We have had it neatly framed and hung up conspicuously in our office.